DEFINING
HR SUCCESS

DEFINING HR SUCCESS

9 Critical Competencies
for HR Professionals

By Kari R. Strobel, James N. Kurtessis,
Debra J. Cohen, and Alexander Alonso

Society for Human Resource Management
Alexandria, Virginia
shrm.org

Society for Human Resource Management
Haidian District Beijing, China
shrm.org/cn

Society for Human Resource Management, India Office
Mumbai, India
shrmindia.org

Society for Human Resource Management, Middle East and Africa Office
Dubai, UAE
shrm.org/pages/mena.aspx

Founded in 1948, the Society for Human Resource Management (SHRM) is the world's largest HR membership organization devoted to human resource management. Representing more than 275,000 members in over 160 countries, the Society is the leading provider of resources to serve the needs of HR professionals and advance the professional practice of human resource management. SHRM has more than 575 affiliated chapters within the United States and subsidiary offices in China, India, and United Arab Emirates. Visit SHRM Online at www.shrm.org.

Interior and Cover Design: Shirley E.M. Raybuck

Library of Congress Cataloging-in-Publication Data

Strobel, Kari R.
  Defining HR success : 9 critical competencies for HR professionals / Kari R. Strobel, James N. Kurtessis, Deb Cohen, and Alexander Alonso.
     pages cm
  Includes bibliographical references and index.
  ISBN 978-1-58644-382-5
  1. Personnel management. I. Title.
  HF5549.S89426 2015
  658.3--dc23
                          2015009792

15-0048

Contents

Foreword

Human resource management, as a profession, is relatively young. It was just over 60 years ago that management guru Peter Drucker published *The Practice of Management* and first used the term "human resources." Since that time, HR has seen substantial change, evolving from a primarily administrative to the strategic business function it is today.

Yet one of our profession's most persistent challenges has been fully articulating what is required to succeed in and deliver great HR.

We knew it when we saw it. We could point to exemplary HR professionals who were business-savvy, well-respected and leading their organization's strategy. They had meaningful relationships with people at every rung of the corporate ladder. They were seen as trusted advisors to the C-suite and the board. They had acquired the leadership mantle reflective of the role human resources plays in the success of organizations. We lifted these individuals up as examples of great HR and where HR needed to go.

But simply knowing *where* HR needs to go is insufficient. To get there expeditiously, we need a roadmap that details *how* to get there and that defines HR success for professionals at every stage of their careers.

SHRM has done that in the *SHRM Competency Model*. We surveyed businesses, educators, and over 32,000 HR professionals to identify the nine critical behavioral and leadership competencies every HR professional needs to succeed and grow. Among the key competencies you'll find in this book are business acumen, leadership and navigation, global and cultural effectiveness and – of course – HR expertise.

These competencies are relevant at every career stage, across all industries, and around the world. They are the behaviors businesses require from modern HR professionals. They are also the competencies demonstrated by the most successful members of the HR profession.

In *Defining HR Success*, you will find information that will help you respond to the new, higher expectations of HR and advance your career to the level business demands. You will find a roadmap to becoming the HR business leader you aspire to be, and to achieving the positive results your organizations needs from HR.

SHRM believes that people are the most critical lever of success in today's fast-paced business environment. We believe that HR must continue to evolve, to lead and drive impact in our organizations. Most important, SHRM believes in *you*.

Henry G. "Hank" Jackson
President & CEO, SHRM

Acknowledgements

The authors would like to thank the following for their contributions in elevating the HR profession:

» Steve Bates
» Brad Boyson
» Tharanga Fonseka
» David Geller
» Lindsay Northon
» Mark J. Schmit
» Rachel Tenenbaum

Your contributions helped make our research better and helped us achieve new heights for defining success in HR.

For the HR profession — your insights represent the most wonderful window into the business world and we are grateful you've shared them with us.

For the Society for Human Resource Management — thank you for taking the bold initiative to advance the profession and for being a true thought leader for today and for tomorrow's HR.

Part I:
Overview and Introduction

The HR profession has been under attack for decades—from "Why We Hate HR" in *Fast Company* to "It's Time to Split HR" in *Harvard Business Review*.[1] Why is this the case? The way in which human resources (employees) are hired, developed, engaged, compensated, and even terminated can have a huge impact on the success or failure of an organization. Yet the way in which HR professionals themselves are selected, developed, and transitioned varies widely across organizations, industries, and countries. In some organizations HR is treated as a key strategic function and accorded the resources and respect needed to be an effective part of the leadership of the organization. In other cases, HR is considered a transactional function with less thought or effort devoted to how the function can both serve the needs of compliance and strategically contribute to the success of the organization; this sense of disrespect is often rooted in business stakeholders even at the educational level.[2] And on this continuum of a transactional function to strategic partner is just about every possibility in between. It is daunting at times to help evolve a profession that has this much variability in practice. Over the years, however, the Society for Human Resource Management (SHRM) has, through its mission, created and executed initiatives to help the profession achieve new heights and evolve the way HR practitioners are viewed, supported, and developed. The SHRM Competency Model is one such initiative. The model defines what it means to be a successful HR practitioner, identifying the critical competencies HR professionals need to solve our most pressing talent issues of today and to deliver HR strategy to enable businesses to evolve into the future.

Chapter 1.

The History of Competency Modeling

To understand the value of the SHRM Competency Model, a brief overview of the history of competency modeling will help set the context for the development of the SHRM model and provide you with a greater understanding of the model's value to you as an HR practitioner and to the HR profession.

What are competencies, and what are competency models?

In a foundational review of competency models, Jeffery S. Shippmann and his colleagues, as delineated by the Society for Industrial and Organizational Psychology (SIOP) taskforce on competency modeling and explored further by Michael Campion and his colleagues, noted a great deal of variability in how competencies are defined, often depending on the professional field of interest and the context of the discussion.[1] When conducting research on the HR profession, SHRM defines a competency as a collection of knowledge, skills, abilities, and other characteristics (KSAOs) that contribute to individual and organizational performance.

A competency model is a set of related competencies linked together that describe the requisite attributes (that is, KSAOs) for successful job performance in a given domain, such as human resources. Competency models include a set of specific behavioral statements that define the competencies and describe what the job-related behavior for each competency looks like. Competencies can be either technical (or functional, capturing the "what" of the job that is being performed) or they can be behavioral (capturing the "how" you perform your job successfully). Both types of competencies, technical and behavioral, should be included in any one competency model (see Figure 1.1). Well-developed and easily implemented competency models typically have no more than 8 to 15 competencies, capturing both the technical skills and behavioral attributes that are needed for successful job performance.[2]

Figure 1.1. Relationship among KSAOs, Competencies, and a Competency Model

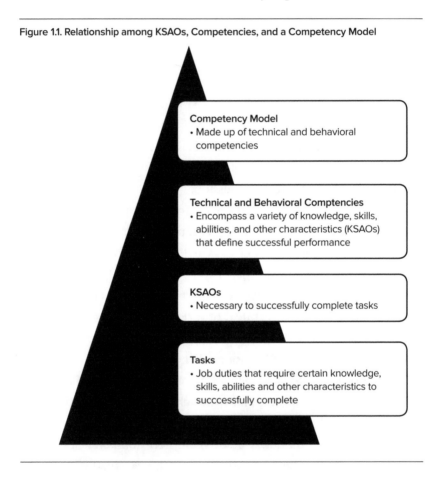

Competency Model
• Made up of technical and behavioral competencies

Technical and Behavioral Comptencies
• Encompass a variety of knowledge, skills, abilities, and other characteristics (KSAOs) that define successful performance

KSAOs
• Necessary to successfully complete tasks

Tasks
• Job duties that require certain knowledge, skills, abilities and other characteristics to succcessfully complete

---

Where did the practice of using competency models come from? The practice of competency modeling was not developed by a single individual or at a specific point in time. Instead, the practice and our current conceptualization of competencies and competency models have evolved slowly over the past 40 years. The work of David McClelland is often viewed as the origin of the current competency movement.[3] McClelland, in an attempt to understand academic achievement testing, presented competencies as an alternative to the then-prevalent approach that focused on traits and intelligence. Subsequent research by Richard E. Boyatzis focused on the "characteristics" of more than 2,000 managers, which were arranged into a management competency model.[4]

The practice of competency modeling also grew from the use of assessment centers, as a method of assessing employee performance and potential to identify managerial-level employees who are ready for promotion or to determine specific training needs. Assessment centers function on the basic idea that a broad set of job-related KSAOs (called "dimensions") are required across similar jobs.[5]

Competency models rest on the assumption that a broad set of job-related competencies can be used to understand and assess employee performance across a variety of jobs and organizations. For example, the competencies necessary for successful performance as an HR generalist in one organization may also be necessary for successful performance as an HR manager in another organization.

The practice of competency modeling gained widespread popularity after the introduction of core competencies in 1990 by C. K. Prahalad and Gary Hamel.[6] They defined "core competencies" as those needed by an organization to operate successfully. Although these thought leaders focused on competencies at the organizational level, which are different from individual employee competencies, they emphasized that an organization's employees are the building blocks that give rise to the organizational-level competencies and thus should be the focus of change initiatives. In other words, an organization's ability to operate successfully and achieve strategic objectives is an outcome of individual employee competencies. Today, HR departments focus on selecting for and training on individual-level competencies to support the attainment of desired business outcomes.[7]

How Competencies Influence Business Outcomes

When we speak about competencies influencing business outcomes, we are talking about both "hard" and "soft" outcomes. Hard outcomes are concrete and quantitative, such as job performance, profit and loss, or turnover; soft outcomes are qualitative and less tangible, for example, the satisfaction and engagement of employees or the reputation of the organization. Because competencies provide reinforcement of the link between organizational goals and workplace behavior, we need to consider these outcomes from two angles: the organization and the individual.

We all crave work that keeps us interested—or "engaged"—in our tasks (a soft outcome at the individual level). The desire to be engaged is innate in almost all of us—especially on the job. When we find ourselves engaged in our job tasks, we are likely to see a spike in our productivity (a hard outcome at the individual level), which may affect pay or benefits. A surge in productivity at the individual level typically translates into cost-effectiveness for the organization (a hard outcome at the organization level[8]). We can then translate the hard outcome of cost-effectiveness into balancing the organization's scorecard and ensuring that the productivity is aligned with the mission and vision of the organization (a soft outcome at the organization level). By informing employees that the organization is on track, the individuals on the team are more likely to experience a flow of self-esteem, perpetuating the cycle of positive business outcomes.

How can an organization come to know the mediators of these outcomes? What are the drivers? Competencies help us answer these questions (see Figure 1.2).

For example, at the core of any job is the conceptual framework of technical or functional competencies. Beyond these technical areas of expertise, behavioral competencies work together to harmonize the organization's well-being with the organizational commitment of its personnel. Technically proficient employees are

Figure 1.2 Desired Business Outcomes

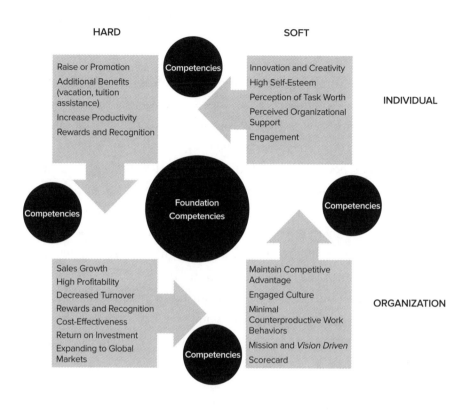

the driving force behind helping the organization be cost-effective and shaping an engaged work culture. Similarly, an HR professional with strong behavioral attributes or competencies will establish programs, policies, and procedures to support the organizational culture so that, at the individual level, employees continue to have high self-esteem and to work toward increased productivity.

Implementing a competency-based talent management strategy helps business professionals answer tough questions:

» What is going well?

» Where do we need to excel?

» Do employees have knowledge gaps or skills gaps that are affecting optimal performance?

» Do we have the tools/resources to do the job?

» What does our organization need to do differently to increase our value to stakeholders?

It is the competencies of the HR professional that work to reconcile how the organization performs today, what the individuals need for tomorrow, and what improvements can be made now to achieve desired business outcomes.

Competencies are the fulcrum of high-performing organizations. For you to effectively contribute to the strategy of the business and be a great business partner, you need to possess not only those competencies that are technical but also those that are behavioral. You also must be able to identify and recognize those competencies that the organization deems important and relevant. The process of effectively and objectively measuring competencies that the organization values against the competencies currently held by individuals within the organization is the key to that company's business success.

Competency Models in Human Resources

Early HR competency models focused on knowledge-specific competencies, such as knowledge of employment law and knowledge of benefits structure, as opposed to more general work-related abilities, such as the ability to manage interpersonal relationships and the ability to provide attention to detail. However, competency modelers realized that HR success requires more than just knowledge; successful HR performance is a combination of KSAOs. Today, competencies integrate KSAOs that indicate what successful employees need to know—knowledge—and what they need to be able to do—skills and abilities.

As previously noted, other HR competency models exist, and SHRM has participated in the data collection with Dave Ulrich and the

RBL Group's HR competency model[9] as well as in the development of other models by Tom Lawson and Vaughan Limbrick.[10] Although these models and discussions have added greatly to our knowledge in the field, nothing has been as comprehensive as the current research to create the SHRM Competency Model. In the past, it made sense to look at various segments of HR (for example, senior and executive). However, if the HR profession is to continue its effort to be taken more seriously by those outside the profession, the entire profession—from education to entry level to executive level—needs to have a robust map, tools, and assessments to help guide the development of critical skills and critical thinkers.

An evidence-based competency model developed by the profession and validated in organizations provides copious opportunities and an ideal place to start for individuals who are entering the profession or who are currently in the profession and seek to enhance their capability and reception in the business community. If the sentiment expressed by chief human resource officers (CHROs) in the 2011 book, *The Chief HR Officer*,[11] is correct, then our efforts to date have not been sufficient in training and preparing future professionals. Those individuals dedicated to the profession have an obligation to improve, not just promote, the skills, abilities, and expertise of HR professionals.

Furthermore, because the field of HR is multifaceted and continually undergoing change, competency models have become broader and more flexible over time. As technology changes the way organizations do business and the way modern workplaces function, the role of the modern HR professional must also change. Prominent HR models[12] show evidence of this constant adaptation, and it is good practice to revise and update any competency model as needed.[13]

You might wonder why researchers put so much effort into maintaining competency models. It is so that changes in business, society, technology, and other factors are reflected to ensure job relevance (see Figure 1.3).

Figure 1.3. Application to HR Practices

HR PROFESSIONALS	ORGANIZATIONS
• Identify your competency strengths and opportunities • Develop a road map for career development • Create your individual development plan • Set performance goals aligned with your competency roadmap • Evaluate your competency development • Advance your HR career	• Assess workforce competency gaps • Implement competency-based recruiting and hiring • Create competency-based training and development • Integrate competencies into career pathing • Expand performance management to include competencies • Advance your organization's HR department

---

For example, competency models are helpful in recruiting employees because they outline the most important qualities to look for in job candidates, given that grades and college and advanced degrees do not fully account for job performance variance.[14] Competencies, on the other hand, are attributes that are tied to successful performers. Knowledge and skill are what distinguish good performance from mediocre performance. Competencies have gained popularity among organizations looking at ways to identify, hire, and retain top talent. Competency models are particularly helpful in finding the right people for senior roles: In recent years, competency models have frequently been used to guide executive succession programs,[15] given that otherwise the qualities of a good executive might be difficult to identify. Competency models often serve as the foundation for defining and identifying improvement areas for current employees and for providing clarity in what content should be covered in an organization's training programs.[16]

A key benefit of competency models is that they can be customized to describe the specific competencies needed at each career level and for different job roles. A competency model may, for example, describe how a specific competency might not be of much importance at the early career level but is essential for senior-level HR professionals. In situations where an employee targeted for potential promotion is failing to develop as expected, managers can use a competency model to identify the competencies that an employee is lacking and can structure development activities to promote growth.[17] Competency models make clear exactly which competencies and, more significantly, which behaviors are of utmost importance for employees wishing to advance their careers.

SHRM's Goals Related to Competencies

The intent from the outset of developing an HR competency model has been to serve the entire HR profession from the college graduate to the executive, looking at the profession holistically and asking: "What do HR professionals need in order to be successful when they begin their careers and as they progress?" This effort connects to other initiatives from SHRM, such as the focus on students and academic curriculum. Advancing the HR profession and providing lifelong career resources is a distinguishing factor for SHRM as the world's largest HR professional society.

Work on the competency model began with examining the career path of HR professionals and determining how their competencies are enhanced over their careers. Since that study, SHRM has sharpened its focus to ensure that it can provide tools for HR professionals to develop themselves. The overarching goal of SHRM's competency modeling initiative is to define what it means to be a successful HR professional. This starts with defining the knowledge and behaviors associated with success.

The foundation of the initiative is the SHRM Competency Model. This model is designed for the entire HR profession: Each competency listed in the model is relevant for all within HR regardless of level, organization size, setting, or specialization. How is that possible? The answer is that these competencies are needed for every job, role, or function in the practice of HR management. The level of expertise needed in each competency will vary according to your role or function or organization, but some level of proficiency in each competency is needed. You might require additional competencies for specialized roles or functions, but these nine competencies serve as the core competencies, to be augmented as necessary. Because of this, the SHRM Competency Model has several features that make it distinct from other HR competency models.

The Model Applies to the Broad Profession and Not Just to Specific Roles or Career Levels

Other models for the HR profession have focused primarily on experienced professionals. The SHRM model is applicable to all career levels. It describes what each competency looks like at each of four career levels: early career, midlevel, senior level, and executive. In addition to helping the HR professional, this model is also useful for business executives outside HR to help them understand what HR does and, more importantly, what to expect from HR.

The Model Is Applicable Regardless of Industry or Organizational Bias

Some competency models are designed for a specific organization or industry, or even for HR professionals within a specific organization or industry. Although these models are useful, they are not applicable across different organizations and industries. For example, a competency model designed for HR professionals in a large, multinational organization might not be applicable to a one-person HR department in a small, regional organization. Unlike other HR competency models, the rigorous and extensive development of the SHRM Competency Model ensures that it is applicable to all HR professionals.

The Model Is Geared for Organizations of All Sizes

Whether you are working in an HR department of one or are part of a large multinational enterprise with 100 HR professionals, the

SHRM model is applicable to your career development. Because SHRM's research included HR professionals from a wide variety of organizational types and sizes, it is broadly applicable.

The Model Is Global in Its Focus
As will be discussed later, the SHRM Competency Model is based on input not only from HR professionals in the U.S. but also from professionals in Africa, Asia, Europe, the Middle East, and South America. In fact, people in 33 nations participated in the development of the competency model, with more than 32,000 HR professionals engaged.

Advantages to Using the SHRM Competency Model

Having a foundational model provides several advantages to the HR practitioner seeking professional development.

It Defines Success as an HR Professional
The SHRM model offers relevant guidance to HR professionals for career development by defining what successful performance looks like. This ensures that HR practitioners can maximize their performance at their current job levels. Because this model defines four career levels, it provides a way for HR professionals to understand how successful job behavior differs across career levels. This, in turn, helps them identify and evaluate their career development. Additionally, SHRM's model makes it easy for HR professionals to grasp what effective on-the-job behavior and performance look like. Behavioral terminology, rather than descriptive terms about roles helps to provide a clear picture of success.

Hiring, and Developing HR Professionals Is Now Easier
Organizations seeking to recruit and develop talented HR professionals now have a clear road map for doing so. By defining

standards for proficiency and key behaviors, the SHRM model helps organizations build successful HR functions. Further, with a clear definition of successful performance, organizations can more easily determine where to allocate resources such as money, time, and attention in the selection, development, and growth of HR business partners.

A Baseline for the Field of HR Management Is Now Available

SHRM's mission is to advance the profession and to serve the professional. That requires an understanding of the current state of the HR profession and where it will be tomorrow. Moreover, the role of a professional society is to set the agenda for the profession and the professional.

The Value of HR to Any Enterprise Is Now More Tangible

A common question encountered by HR professionals is, "What is my return on investment, or ROI, for HR initiatives?" This calls for HR practitioners to be able to analyze their initiatives and activities and communicate their contributions to the organization's success in tangible, measurable outcomes. We offer that this model provides the foundation to communicate how HR contributes to organizational success. It does so with a clear definition of what HR does and how it adds value to organizations.

Best Practices in Competency Model Development

Because competency models contain a vast amount of information, developing a model is a time- and labor-intensive process. For guidance in developing a robust competency model, SHRM followed a set of specific guidelines offered by the Society for Industrial and Organizational Psychology (SIOP), Division 14 of the American Psychological Association (APA).[18] According to these guidelines, developing a strong competency model requires

three distinct phases:
1. Compiling the content of the model using job analysis methods.
2. Evaluating and revising the content of the model through content-related validity studies.
3. Assessing how the model relates to job performance through criterion-related validity studies.

Phase 1: Developing and Revising the Straw Model

Though it seems somewhat obvious, developing a competency model begins with compiling as much information as possible about the nature of HR jobs from existing resources. To do this, SHRM created an initial competency model by reviewing and integrating information from academic sources, such as academic journal articles, and from industry literature, such as technical reports from consulting organizations, about the jobs of HR professionals. In addition, SHRM surveyed 640 chief human resource officers (CHROs) and asked what they, and their direct reports, needed to know and do to be successful on the job (see Appendix A). SHRM referred to this initial model as the "straw model."

An important aspect of the straw model was the identification of four career levels for HR professionals: early career, mid, senior, and executive. Table 1.1 provides a general description of the four career levels. These career levels reflect the varying types of responsibilities for which HR professionals are accountable. Specifically, early career levels (i.e., early career and mid-level) reflect responsibilities that are more transactional in nature, whereas more senior levels (i.e., senior and executive levels) reflect responsibilities that are more strategic in nature. These career levels were created to reflect the fact that the job of HR professionals differs qualitatively across career levels, a concept incorporated into and reflected in the final SHRM Competency Model.

Table 1.1. HR Professional Career Levels and Descriptions

Career Level	Typical Characteristics
Early	• Is a specialist in a specific support function, or is a generalist with limited experience. • Holds a formal title such as HR assistant, junior recruiter, or benefits clerk.
Mid	• Is a generalist or a senior specialist. • Manages projects or programs. • Holds a formal title such as HR manager, generalist, or senior specialist.
Senior	• Is a very experienced generalist or specialist. • Holds a formal title such as senior manager, director, or principal.
Executive	• Typically is one of the most senior leaders in HR. • Holds the top HR job in the organization or a VP role.

Following the development of the straw model, SHRM staff traveled to 29 cities across the globe to refine and enhance the straw model using subject matter experts from the field of HR (see Appendix B). Over 1,200 HR professionals participated in 111 focus groups. During these focus group sessions, HR professionals edited the model and added or modified it when they believed that certain aspects of the job were not captured accurately enough. Using this process, the subject matter experts began to converge on a finished draft of a model that was then transitioned to the content validation phase.

Phase 2: Competencies and Job Relatedness

Although referencing existing resources and gaining input from subject matter experts are necessary in the early stages of developing a strong competency model, qualitative research is not enough. The Uniform Guidelines on Employee Selection Procedures by the U.S. Equal Employment Opportunity Commission[19] and the *Principles for the Validation and Use of Personnel Selection Procedures* developed by SIOP2003 (and updated in 2012) explain that the content of the model must be subjected to quantitative evaluation—a process known as content validation. To investigate the validity of the model's content, SHRM researchers developed and launched the largest content validation research survey in the Society's history. Over 32,000 HR professionals responded, making it the largest cross-sectional survey in the history of HR competencies research.

This survey collected information from HR professionals about the accuracy, relevance, and importance of the competency model's content. Based on these data, SHRM revised the model where needed, for example, by adding or removing behaviors that describe individual competencies. In total, HR professionals in 33 nations contributed to the processes of model development and content validation. Findings from our content validation survey will be discussed throughout the remainder of the book; however, for more technical information on SHRM's content validation research, see Appendix B.

Phase 3: Proficiency and Performance

The final step in developing a strong competency model is to evaluate the extent to which the model is associated with job performance. After all, a competency model is supposed to be a comprehensive resource that describes the attributes needed by HR professionals to be successful. To test this aspect of SHRM's model, SHRM conducted a criterion validation study to examine the link between proficiency in the competencies and job performance for HR professionals.[21] The study was undertaken to add to the extensive validity evidence, collected from more than 32,000 SHRM members and HR professionals, which supports the content of the model as applicable to and reflective of the job of HR professionals.

To examine the link between competencies and job performance, SHRM collected data from four corporate partners and four academic partners that were awarded grants through the SHRM Foundation. To measure the competencies, study participants completed several assessments, including a behavioral self-report assessment and a situational judgment test. These assessments were rigorously developed and tested to accurately measure the SHRM Competency Model. In total, more than 1,513 participants completed these assessments. SHRM also collected job performance ratings with a scale designed specifically for this study. In total, both participant data and supervisor performance ratings were available for almost 900 participants.

The results of this study indicate that a higher level of proficiency on the SHRM Competency Model is related to higher levels of job performance. In other words, employees who have more developed competencies are viewed by supervisors as performing at a higher level on the job. Additionally, the behavioral competencies in the SHRM model were associated with higher levels of job performance even after controlling for participants' HR knowledge. Overall, results demonstrate that the competencies, as a set, account for variance in job performance and that the behavioral competencies account for variance in job performance above and beyond both demographic characteristics (e.g., education and years of job experience) and HR knowledge.

Combined with evidence supporting the content validity of the SHRM Competency Model, the criterion validity evidence provides strong support for the model as a valid and useful blueprint for success as an HR professional.

Part II:
The SHRM Competency Model: Foundational Competencies

The SHRM Competency Model comprises nine competencies that HR professionals need in order to be successful. One technical competency—*HR Expertise (HR Knowledge)*—describes major elements of work within the HR profession:

» Talent acquisition and retention.

» Employee engagement.

» Learning and development.

» Total rewards.

» Structure of the HR function.

» Organizational effectiveness and development.

» Workforce management.

» Employee relations.

» Technology and data.

» HR in the global context.

» Diversity and inclusion.

» Risk management.

» Corporate social responsibility.

» Employment law regulations.

» Business and HR strategy.

Eight behavioral competencies define how you apply your fundamental skills as an HR professional to become a strategic business partner:

» Ethical practice.

» Communication.

» Leadership and navigation.

» Relationship management.

» Consultation.

» Critical evaluation.

» Business acumen.

» Global and cultural effectiveness.

The model in its entirety speaks to how you as an HR professional provide and demonstrate the greatest value to your organization. *HR Expertise (HR Knowledge)* includes subject areas that are fundamental to HR operations. You might specialize in one or a few of them. And you might approach them differently whether you are new to the field, are at midcareer, have reached senior status, or have become a top HR executive. But they are the core disciplines. The eight behavioral competencies provide the direction to help you become a strategic business partner within your organization. In combination, both competency types provide the road map needed to help you build your career.

Chapter 2.

HR Expertise (HR Knowledge)

HR Expertise (HR Knowledge)—referred to as *HR Expertise* throughout the remainder of this book—describes the technical areas of expertise that HR professionals develop and hone over time not only to serve the needs of the talent within the organization but also to strategically align the practices of HR professionals to where the organization needs to go in the future. HR professionals directly affect organizational success by developing, maintaining, and executing sound human resource management (HRM) policies, practices, and procedures[1] that support organizational mission and goals. Effective HRM practices are critical for success. Among a few of the numerous benefits: reduced turnover, increased productivity and financial performance, and sustained competitive advantage.[2] To implement successful initiatives, HR professionals must have well-developed knowledge and skill in performing effective HRM practice; this is reflected in the *HR Expertise* competency.

Human Resource Expertise is defined as the knowledge of principles, practices, and functions of effective human resource management.

Through its specificity to the HR profession, *HR Expertise* describes the knowledge, skills, abilities, and behaviors needed by HR professionals to design, enact, evaluate, and maintain sound HRM practices. It also includes the policies, practices, laws/regulations, and principles that underlie effective HRM practices.

Develop Your HR Expertise

There are many ways for HR professionals to develop their expertise. Multiple activities should be undertaken continuously over time to develop, maintain, and extend professional expertise. Below are some examples of how to develop HR expertise.

- Seek out a mentor who possesses expertise in areas you wish to develop.
- Enroll in a course at a local college or university.
- Participate in workshops, conferences, and training opportunities internal and external to your organization.
- Study for a certification exam and become certified.
- Volunteer to work on a project or assignment in an area of HR you are not as familiar with to further develop your knowledge.
- Take notes during meetings, and identify questions to ask your manager.
- Shadow a senior-level employee.
- Identify areas of strength and opportunities for development within your HR department.
- Pay attention to current events and developments relevant to HR practice.
- Study departmental resources to gain knowledge relevant to your desired areas of development.
- Engage in self-directed learning through books, seminars, and/or educational opportunities.

As a technical competency, *HR Expertise* serves as the driver of behavioral competencies, such as *Business Acumen, Critical Evaluation*, and *Consultation*. For example, an HR professional might convey his or her knowledge about effective HRM practices through a behavioral competency such as *Communication* or *Consultation*.

HR Expertise comprises several functional areas to include talent acquisition and retention, employee engagement, learning and development, total rewards, structure of the HR function, organizational effectiveness and development, workforce management, employee relations, technology and data, HR in the global context, diversity and inclusion, risk management, corporate social responsibility, employment law regulations, and business and HR strategy. These 15 functional areas compose the *HR Expertise* functional areas within SHRM's Body of Competency and Knowledge (BoCK), which documents the HR behavioral competencies and knowledge domains tested on the SHRM Certified Professional (SHRM-CP) and SHRM Senior Certified Professional (SHRM-SCP) certification exams. A detailed discussion centered on SHRM's BoCK and certification exams is presented in Chapter 13.[3]

Those functional areas that focus on HR as a talent management discipline and include talent acquisition and retention, employee engagement, learning and development, total rewards, and employment law and regulations highlight KSAOs (knowledge, skills, abilities, and other characteristics) that a highly proficient HR professional needs for success on the job. Activities associated with HR as a discipline in effectively managing an organization's talent include the following:

» Acquiring talent by developing, implementing, and measuring the individual and organizational success of employee sourcing, recruiting, hiring, onboarding, orientation, and retention activities and programs.

» Understanding and leveraging the employer-employee relationship from both the individual and organizational perspective and developing effective strategies to address appropriate performance and behavioral expectations for employees at all levels.

» Identifying or creating training and development opportunities that increase employee capability and organizational knowledge.

» Designing and administering compensation and benefit systems and programs (base pay, incentive pay, benefits, leaves, retirement, and perquisites) that support attraction and retention efforts.

» Ensuring compliance with laws and regulations both on a domestic and global basis, including those that apply on an extraterritorial basis.

The most useful component of the *HR Expertise* competency is its proficiency standards in which an HR professional at the relevant career level should engage to be successful. The model acknowledges that success for an early HR professional is defined and executed differently from that of a senior HR professional. For example, at earlier career levels, HR professionals proficient in *HR Expertise* develop knowledge of general HR practices and technology; execute transactions with minimal errors; generate and, when appropriate, implement solutions with designated areas of responsibility; and follow relevant laws and regulations. By contrast, demonstrating mastery of *HR Expertise* at the executive level includes aligning the delivery of HR services to proactively integrate with organizational initiatives, assessing business situations and developing strategies to improve organizational performance, providing balanced long- and short-term strategic vision, overseeing HR issues involving legal and financial risk to organizations, and educating and advising the executive team on strategic HR issues as a factor in decision-making.

As seen in the behavioral standards for executive HR professionals, *HR Expertise* acknowledges that HR is more than just a people business (the day-to-day transactional work performed by HR). To solve our most pressing business issues of today and to deliver HR strategy to enable businesses to evolve in the future, the savvy HR professional needs to:

» Know how to provide HR-related business services that create and drive organizational effectiveness.

» Understand stakeholder needs and the impact of decisions to the overall workforce.

» Align the organizational vision, mission, and goals with day-to-day operational activities, including organizational design, development, performance measures, and standards.

» Manage the workforce effectively to addresses the ability of the organization to meet the critical people needs and gaps through strategic activities (for example, workforce planning, succession planning).

» Ensure the appropriate framework, mindset, and practices are in place to embrace, react, or respond to employee representation.

» Deal effectively with the use of tools, machines, and systems.

» Focus on organizational growth and workforce-related issues and impacts, from a domestic, multinational, and global perspective.

» Implement policies, programs, and assessments that mitigate situations or circumstances that have the potential to cause business disruption.

Recalling the content validation survey we discussed when describing how the model was developed, we found that *HR Expertise* was rated as "critical" (without this competency HR professionals *could not perform* their jobs at even a minimally acceptable level, which could result in major consequences on overall effectiveness) to the successful performance of both executive- and senior-level practitioners, whereas early- and midcareer-level practitioners rated *HR Expertise* as "important" (without this competency HR professionals *would have difficulty performing* their jobs effectively, which could result in consequences on overall effectiveness). On the whole, HR professionals rated *HR Expertise* as "important" or "critical" to job success, although this competency is viewed as most important at more senior career levels than at junior career levels. Presumably, this discrepancy occurs as the result of an increase in responsibility, the expansion of managerial responsibilities, and a move from transactional to more strategic job responsibilities. It is also possible that early-career-level professionals are expected to develop this competency through on-the-job training or more formalized training and educational opportunities (for example, conferences, workshops). These career level differences suggest that the *HR Expertise* competency is important across all career levels and becomes more important, and a requisite qualification, at more senior career levels.

For HR Managers

- Assign mentors who possess expertise in areas that need to be developed.
- Require participation in workshops, conferences, and training opportunities internal and external to your organization.
- Require HR certification for managers.
- Use stretch assignments to help your employees acquire new skills.

Chapter 3.
Ethical Practice

HR management centers on fairness and justice for an organization's most valuable resource, its people. In other words, HR management is all about ethics, ethical principles, and ethical practice. Ethical Practice is defined as the integration of integrity and accountability throughout all organizational and business practices.

Ethical Practice is the ability to integrate core values, integrity, and accountability throughout all organizational and business practices.

As with all other employees, HR professionals should behave ethically. They must consider the core values of their organizations and act with integrity. But beyond adhering to rigorous ethical standards themselves, HR professionals are often tasked with creating ethical HR systems or reinforcing an organization's ethical climate.

HR departments often serve as the one-stop shop for employment practices, operations information, and legal questions. Because everyone is processed through HR and because the department is frequently in charge of implementing and educating about new policies, HR professionals promote, encourage, and educate ethical behavior in the workplace. These efforts serve several purposes, but most notably are that implementing a strong ethical climate can help protect an organization from adverse employee behavior

Develop Your Ethical Practice

There are many ways for HR professionals to develop their expertise. Multiple activities should be undertaken continuously over time to develop, maintain, and extend professional expertise. Below are some examples of how to develop ethical practices.

- Seek out opportunities to build trust with coworkers through honesty and consistency.
- Attend an ethics workshop internal or external to your organization.
- Review internal and external policies relevant to your day-to-day HR responsibilities.
- Take the time to stay up-to-date on compliance practices.
- Familiarize yourself with the application of ethical policies within your organization.
- Seek out a mentor who serves as a role model of ethical behavior and standards.
- Take the initiative to demonstrate ethical behavior to others in your department.
- Volunteer to serve on an ethics counsel or board.
- Assist in the investigation of an ethical concern.
- Develop or participate in internal or external ethics training.
- Set aside time to engage in self-directed learning on emerging ethical trends and practices.

and that implementing ethical systems is essential to organizations because ethical HR systems are associated with higher levels of organizational performance.[1]

HR professionals at all career levels can not only adhere to their organizations' ethical climate but help drive it as well. For example, early- and midcareer-level practitioners might be responsible for conducting thorough and confidential investigations into reports of unethical behavior and recommending further action (for example, suspension or termination of an employee). At more senior levels of experience, HR professionals might be responsible for ensuring that HR systems reinforce appropriate employee behaviors, values, and norms that contribute to the organization's ethical climate. For example, senior-level HR professionals might develop effective policies and procedures for employees to report unethical behavior or ensure that the requirements for determining promotions and pay raises are consistent throughout the organization and transparent for employees. Successful HR practitioners adhere to ethical guidelines with regard to their own behavior and also serve as drivers of an ethical climate in their organizations. To do this, HR employees must have thoroughly developed competence in *Ethical Practice*.

So what does having thoroughly developed competence in *Ethical Practice* mean? Our research suggests that HR professionals who are highly proficient in this critical competency domain build trust and rapport among their peers, subordinates, leadership, and colleagues. In addition, they maintain the highest personal, professional, and behavioral integrity, are credible, and display both personal and professional courage in times of crisis. Specifically they do the following:

» Maintain confidentiality.

» Act with personal, professional, and behavioral integrity.

» Respond immediately to all reports of unethical behavior or conflicts of interest.

» Empower all employees to report unethical behavior or conflicts of interest without fear of reprisal.

» Show consistency between espoused and enacted values.

» Acknowledge mistakes.

» Drive the corporate ethical environment.

» Apply power or authority appropriately.

» Recognize personal bias and others' tendency toward bias, and take measures to mitigate the influence of bias in business decisions.

» Maintain appropriate levels of transparency in organizational practices.
» Ensure that all stakeholder voices are heard.
» Manage political and social pressures when making decisions.

But are ethics really that important?

In meetings with over 1,200 practitioners worldwide, ethical practice was clearly seen as a principal behavior demanded of all HR professionals, and reputation and credibility will always be important, whether as a full-time employee, an independent contractor, a task-based service provider, or an ad hoc provider.

In addition, our content validation survey results indicate that this competency was rated as "critical" to the performance of HR professionals at all career levels, with ratings increasing slightly with career level, suggesting that *Ethical Practice* is essential to job success at all career levels.

For some, maintaining your reputation and credibility may be about providing a professional service to the employer. For others, the issues go beyond professionalism: You may feel that your practice extends to questions about how to behave, based on moral duties and virtues arising from principles about right and wrong.

Ethical issues—how they are recognized, understood, and managed—can enhance professional reputation, personal credibility, and client service, or result in a disciplinary inquiry into the practitioner's conduct as an employee or the termination of a long-term service contract. The way to take advantage of the benefits and to avoid the pitfalls is to become ethically aware. Many HR professionals face ethical issues and over time have gained the experience and the insight to work them out in ways that have fair and moral outcomes for all.

You can and will encounter many ethical dilemmas. The key is to be able to recognize an ethical issue, and to respond to it, with the behaviors previously mentioned as your guide for how to respond appropriately.

For HR Managers

- Provide opportunities to discuss ethical dilemmas among HR staff to better understand issues as they may relate to your organization.

- Practice in developing a code of ethics and then applying it to situations to establish an ethical business image.

- Practice ethical decision making and reflect on your skills as an HR professional with the exercises and case studies.

- Make ethics a clear and consistent part of your agendas, set standards, model appropriate behavior, and hold everyone accountable.

Part III:

The SHRM Competency Model: Business Competencies

Technical expertise only gets you so far. To be successful in HR you need to be more than technically proficient. You need to translate what you know through key behavioral competencies. The combination of technical expertise and behaviors provides the right formula for success as an HR professional and as a business person. In today's challenging business environment the workforce provided by HR should align with and meet the needs of the business strategy. Now HR professionals are expected to be valued team members with the rest of the organization and contribute as business partners for the growth of the organization. The HR Strategic Business Partner now serves the purpose of providing *HR Expertise* and behavioral attributes to organizational resources to contribute more strategically to business goals.

HR professionals are equipped with the KSAOs and talent to partner with senior leadership not only to be involved in the strategic management of the organization but to drive the implementation of it. HR strategic business partners are effective at building strong partnerships with senior leaders as they provide expert advice on all matters relating to the ongoing development of the organization. How do they do it? They have the ability to (a) understand and apply information to contribute to the organization's strategic plan, (b) interpret information to make business decisions and recommendations, and (c) provide guidance to organizational stakeholders. In other words, these successful HR practitioners are highly proficient in three critical HR strategic partner competencies: *Business Acumen, Critical Evaluation,* and *Consultation.* These three competencies highlight the shift from transactional to strategic HR, and describe those behavioral attributes to which you must apply your HR lens to drive organizational strategy.

Chapter 4.

Business Acumen

We have all heard about business acumen for years. *Business Acumen* is the primary skill needed for making a strategic contribution to the business. What we can say from our research is that proficient HR professionals are practitioners who think in terms of the business and operations first and then apply the HR lens to their work. Specifically, the ability to understand all business functions within the organization and industry is a core component of becoming an HR business operator. This requires a strategic focus with systems thinking and economic awareness based on four areas of knowledge: business administration, finance, marketing, and operations expertise. In our travels, we encountered numerous adept practitioners. The common thread among them was the ability to understand how the business makes money and what operations best support the mission of the organization. Similarly, these professionals were then able to draw a link between HR metrics and business outcomes like key performance indicators (KPIs).

Business Acumen is defined as the ability to understand and apply information with which to contribute to the organization's strategic plan.

Developing *Business Acumen* is required of HR professionals to participate and help the organization be competitive. Learning more about their company's financial results, understanding the numbers, and, more importantly, knowing how their decisions and

Learn the Business

There are many way for HR professionals to develop their expertise. Multiple activities should be undertaken continuously over time to develop, maintain, and extend professional expertise. Below are some examples of how to develop business acumen.

- Read books, magazines, and newspapers on topics such as business practices, marketing, entrepreneurism, negotiation, and economics.
- Join a professional or industry association.
- Enroll in business continuing education courses.
- Participate in company projects, committees, or special initiatives.
- Work on a cross-functional team with colleagues from finance, accounting, marketing, or operations.
- Study your company's financial statements to develop a comprehensive understanding of what drives profitability and cash flow.
- Analyze and synthesize market and competitive data.
- Know and monitor your organization's key performance indicators (KPIs).
- Seek out a mentor who possesses expertise in areas you wish to develop.

actions affect the bottom line will help contribute to the success of the organization. Those HR professionals proficient in business acumen understand how to improve their alignment with the organization's financial performance, innovation, and market-value goals; they are aware of their own impact on financial outcomes and understand how their behavior affects value-creating activities in the organization and, in turn, understand the impact their behavior has on gross margin. In short, successful HR practitioners, high on *Business Acumen,* make behavioral and process changes helping to increase the gross margin impact of their actions and decisions. These individuals are seen as fellow business partners and not necessarily as "HR."

For example, as an HR professional, you are responsible for developing a comprehensive strategic workforce plan that plays a vital role in the achievement of your organization's overall strategic objectives and visibly illustrates that the HR function fully understands and supports the direction in which the organization wants to go. The workforce plan that you develop outlines having the right talent in the right place at the right time, three to seven years out, that supports other strategic objectives undertaken by marketing, financial, operational, and technology departments. Through your understanding of the "business," your workforce plan will add value to the organization by articulating more clearly how the acquisition, development, and even termination of employees support the achievement of other plans and strategies, and by identifying fundamental underlying issues that must be addressed by the organization if its employees are to be motivated and committed and are to operate effectively (i.e., engagement).

As you can see, HR practitioners can have a major impact on business outcomes through their understanding of the relationships between HR functions, metrics, and business operations. But what does *Business Acumen* look like in practice? How do you know if you are engaging in those successful behaviors required of this critical competency domain? Beyond discussing why this competency is important and how it is defined, let us show you what you need to do to develop business savvy and sense to make good judgments and quick decisions. From our discussions with thousands of HR experts around the world, we found that those HR professionals who are highly proficient in *Business Acumen* effectively and routinely:

» Demonstrate an understanding of the strategic relationship between effective HR management and core business functions.
» Demonstrate a capacity for understanding the business operations and functions within the organization.

» Understand the industry and business/competitive environment within which the organization operates.

» Make the business case for HR management (for example, return on investment, or ROI) as it relates to efficient and effective organizational functioning.

» Understand organizational metrics and their correlation to business success.

» Use organizational resources to learn the business and operational functions.

» Use organizational metrics to make decisions.

» Market HR both internally (for example, ROI of HR initiatives) and externally (for example, employment branding).

» Leverage technology to solve business problems.

» Demonstrate courage and confidence by suggesting ways in which the business can thrive and grow through HR practices *and* through other business practices.

When HR professionals demonstrate these behaviors, they begin to think and act like business owners, focusing on cutting waste and not just costs and indirectly helping to create a culture of accountability within the organization. This participation helps increase HR professionals' motivation and engagement because they know that their efforts really matter.

Our content validation survey reflected the high level of importance placed on *Business Acumen*. Looking at the importance of *Business Acumen* in greater detail, we found that importance values differed by career levels. Specifically, we found both senior and executive-level HR professionals deem *Business Acumen* significantly more important than early- and midcareer-level practitioners, with senior and executive-level professionals placing more value on the importance of *Business Acumen* to their success and the successful contribution to organizational goals and values. This outcome suggests not only that *Business Acumen* is a fundamental competency for all HR professionals but that it is also critical at later stages in one's career.

Overall, developing your business acumen proficiency takes time, and implementing career-level training and developmental opportunities will help you develop proficiency in this business partner competency. What is unique about this competency model is that we have identified proficiency standards for each competency that an HR professional should target to be successful at early, mid, senior, and executive levels. In general, the early-career level is all about developing knowledge, and the executive level is about developing the business strategy and defining the chief business and HR metrics for gauging success. To develop your *Business Acumen*, we have given you the guide—through the identification of behavioral standards set at your current career level and your target career level—to help you identify what you need to focus on to develop the ability to understand business functions and metrics within your organization and industry.

HR experts were clear in their communication that successful performance of Business Acumen looks and feels different at different career levels, with each career level having its own set of "shifting" behavioral standards communicating what successful HR performance looks like from early to executive levels; each set of standards builds on the other to provide the foundation for increasing your proficiency.

Taking a closer look at a set of shifting proficiency standards across career levels, on the topic of developing your understanding of HR metrics and their relationship to critical business outcomes, early-career HR professionals should focus on developing their basic knowledge of HR metrics, whereas midcareer HR professionals need to shift from developing basic knowledge to applying their knowledge of HR metrics to define HR activities in terms of their quantifiable value added, impact, and utility from a cost-benefit analysis perspective. As HR professionals take on more responsibility and confront greater business challenges, those in senior and executive positions most proficient in *Business Acumen* (developed upon previously acquired knowledge and experience at early- and midcareer levels) focus on ensuring that all HR initiatives have ROI that adds to organizational value and develop HR business strategies to drive desired business results.

But developing your business acumen is not enough; we found through our discussions with experts that those with the highest *Business Acumen* were able to use their knowledge of the business coupled with their skills in *Critical Evaluation* to actively identify potential inefficiencies and unrealized revenues (see Appendix B).

For HR Managers

- Assist with setting up round-table discussions for HR managers with functional managers from across the organization to promote understanding and awareness of the business issues facing the organization.
- Provide opportunities for team members to work on cross-functional projects.
- Identify job rotation opportunities across departments.
- Routinely share key performance indicators to help your team evaluate success in reaching business targets.

Chapter 5.
Critical Evaluation

According to 640 chief human resource officers (CHROs), *Critical Evaluation* is the second most important competency behind *Business Acumen* (see Appendix A). As defined, *Critical Evaluation* is the ability to interpret information to make business decisions and recommendations. Otherwise stated, critical evaluation is the skill to digest large amounts of data and assess value to your work and to your organization.

Critical Evaluation is defined as the ability to interpret information with which to make business decisions and recommendations.

HR can enhance the effectiveness and usefulness of HR programs by informing their development and monitoring their success with appropriate data. One such source of data is human capital metrics—for example, metrics that describe the time to fill a position and the cost per hire. Not only do human capital metrics add value to the role of HR in organizations,[1] but HR functions that collect and properly use HR metrics to inform HR activity are seen as more reliable strategic partners.[2] On a more strategic level, the rise of data-based HR management (HRM) practices is clearly evident—one such example of this trend is "big data" and its increasingly frequent use by HR departments. HR professionals are currently being asked to inform their decisions with data, and this

Developing Critical Thinking

There are many ways for HR professionals to develop their expertise. Multiple activities should be undertaken continuously over time to develop, maintain, and extend professional expertise. Below are some examples of how to develop critical thinking skills.

- Debate different points of view.
- Keep current on your professional areas of expertise.
- Formulate an argument by developing points in a logical sequence that leads to a conclusion.
- Look at both strengths and weaknesses.
- Ensure any argument, findings, or results are backed by valid evidence.
- Write objectively, detaching emotion from points of view.
- Develop knowledge of HR metrics.
- Enroll in a formal statistics or research methods course.
- Be a devil's advocate.

trend is likely to continue and increase in the coming years. Data and its analysis can inform and drive HR decisions that influence the performance of the entire organization.

Because of these trends in the HR profession, HR professionals should have the proficiency necessary to collect, analyze, and interpret data and research to inform evidence-based HR management (HRM) practices. To do this, HR professionals must not only understand what data are useful (for example, HR metrics) and how they should be collected (for example, via surveys or archival records), but they must also be able to effectively analyze and interpret those data. In short, HR professionals must be able to translate raw data and research into conclusions relevant to their organizations and then create actionable recommendations that inform HRM practices. To accomplish these tasks, *Critical Evaluation* is an essential competency for HR professionals that we expect to increase in importance in the coming years.

Outsiders to HR, and even those within the profession, often think that an HR professional goes into HR because he or she is not great with numbers or that he or she is a people person. This perception is not accurate. The truth is that HR is all about numbers, metrics, statistics, and research. The truly proficient HR practitioner has a mastery of measurement and assessment, critical thinking, and research design with the expressed aim of answering workforce and business questions. We found that a genuine level of curiosity and inquisitiveness, while maintaining objectivity in the evaluation of data, is a key component to this linchpin business partner competency. Let's dig deeper and evaluate what it takes to be a successful critical evaluator.

We asked HR experts around the globe to tell us how HR practitioners successfully translate raw data, information, and research into conclusions relevant to their organizations and create actionable recommendations that inform HRM practices. This is what they told us: First and foremost, evaluate the evidence. Analyze your data with a keen sense for what is useful by filtering out the noise, apply critical thinking to any and all information received from organizational stakeholders, and evaluate what data can be used to inform and drive organizational success.

The data and information must be examined for hidden weaknesses and flaws, for example, you might question your ability to apply the data that comes from only a few employees to the entire organization. Even if the data seem convincing at first, critically evaluating and analyzing the data may expose limitations or errors. To do this, you need to analyze information to identify evidence-based best practices but also delineate (for yourself) a clear set of best practices based on experience, evidence from industry literature, published peer-reviewed research, publicly available web-based sources of information, and other sources. Know your technical areas of expertise based on your training and experience, and anticipate and identify leading indicators of outcomes. Using your knowledge, skills, and experience, you can critically weigh and judge the evidence for yourself and analyze large quantities of information from research and practice.

Second, view the topic or issue from a variety of angles and perspectives. This is an example of the Socratic method, named after Socrates and his use of dialogue to explore a specific topic. The point of the dialogue is to present different definitions or viewpoints on the issue. A definition is presented, discussed, and debated. The goal of the method is to arrive at the true definition. This is done by diagnosing the inadequacies or weaknesses of definitions until the true definition reveals itself.

Third, continue analyzing an issue or topic until you have a good grasp and can understand the details. Transfer knowledge and best practices from one situation to the next, and gather additional necessary information to help you make sound decisions based on evaluation of available information.

Recalling what we said earlier regarding knowing your technical areas of expertise and using your knowledge, skills, and experience to critically weigh and judge the evidence for yourself, how can you sufficiently evaluate data at early- and midcareer levels if the foundation for success on this competency is built on extensive knowledge and experience? Good question.

What makes the SHRM Competency Model highly useful is its shifting proficiency standards at all HR career levels, providing HR practitioners with behavioral standards to target in an effort to become more proficient in any one competency at the appropriate level. Early-career HR professionals can become proficient in critically evaluating data and information sooner in their careers by entering data and tracking statistics and metrics, whereas midlevel HR professionals can become successful critical evaluators by analyzing these data and reporting findings and trends. At senior and executive levels, HR professionals who are able to identify key messages from research, pilot study findings, and best practices and to make decisions with confidence based on the analysis of these data to drive business success have mastered the skill of critical evaluation at the highest levels.

We know that CHROs are big fans of critical evaluation, but what do other HR professionals think? When analyzing the data from our content validation survey results, we found critical evaluation high on everyone's importance list. HR professionals at all career levels indicated that *Critical Evaluation* is meaningful to job success. However, the importance ratings of this competency increase with career level, such that this competency is rated as more important for more senior career levels than for junior career levels. This finding indicates that HR professionals at early- and midcareer levels are expected to develop *Critical Evaluation* through on-the-job experience and formal training opportunities to advance their careers.

To help you get where you need to go, the shifting proficiency standards become even more important as a pathway to success as you develop within your HR career. Focus, at the outset, on those proficiency standards at early- and midcareer levels to help you become a master at *Critical Evaluation* at later stages in your career, where you will need it most, to make the biggest impact.

Let's think of a practical application. HR professionals can use industry HR measurement data to critically evaluate their organization against competitors or other similar organizations. For example, practitioners can compare their organization's health care costs with similar organizations to see if the discrepancy is large enough to warrant further analysis. Industry HR data also protects areas or programs that are performing well. To illustrate, if line executives want recruiting costs lowered, HR data may show that their current recruiting costs are in line with their industry. In fact, to lower costs far below their competitors might actually jeopardize their organizations' ability to find the right talent to compete in the market.

As you can see, HR professionals need to not only understand what data is useful (e.g., HR metrics) and how it should be collected (e.g., via surveys or archival records) but must also be able to effectively analyze and interpret that data. Moreover, they need to drive when and how data is employed and be able to initiate new or extended uses of data to drive organizational success.

We have discussed the importance of developing both your *Business Acumen* and your *Critical Evaluation* skills to becoming an effective business partner; however, we have yet to talk about how HR professionals through their understanding of the business and interpretation of data can provide guidance to clients and stakeholders as internal consultants.

For HR Managers

- Create a regular data discussion for HR managers to evaluate existing metrics and discuss the value and viability of alternative metrics or analytics that might benefit the organization.
- Provide opportunities to use quantitative and qualitative data as a part of decision making.
- Encourage healthy debate.
- Ask for comparing and contrasting points of view when discussing solutions to business problems.

Chapter 6.

Consultation

HR professionals often serve in a consultative role for other organizational members and business units. This consultative role may include developing and carrying out HR management (HRM) practices that support and are aligned with business strategies and goals. In other words, successful HR professionals develop HR systems that positively contribute to organizational success.[1]

As a consultant, HR professionals can help their organizations address challenges related to HR, such as staffing needs, training and development needs, employee performance issues, and employee relations matters.[2] Successful HR business partners must not only possess requisite knowledge about HRM practices but also be able to provide guidance to internal stakeholders, which is not an easy task.

The most effective HR professionals possess a special set of attributes that enables them to translate complicated information about HRM practices (that is, *HR Expertise*) into actionable recommendations for end-users (for example, hiring managers). Above all, HR practitioners need to know what their clients are talking about. They need expertise about the question, problem, or situation presented to them. Through formal or informal training and development, HR professionals are trained in a specific function or specialty, and it is through the development of this expertise that HR professionals become the "go-to" professionals for help and advice on HR problems and solutions. Ultimately, the foundation for building consulting skills requires some expertise. *Consultation*, within the model, is defined as the ability to provide guidance to organizational stakeholders.

Consultation is defined as the ability to provide guidance to organizational stakeholders.

Become an Internal Consultant

There are many ways for HR professionals to develop their expertise. Multiple activities should be undertaken continuously over time to develop, maintain, and extend professional expertise. Below are some examples of how to develop consultative competencies.

- Shadow a professional in the role of and internal or external consultant.
- Build relationships with clients, colleagues, and stakeholders.
- Ask questions during data gathering meetings with clients and stakeholders.
- Outline client goals, and set expectations for success.
- Apply tools to analyze business needs, and gather information.
- Build credibility through communication to increase your position as a knowledgeable, client-focused partner.
- Overcome resistance and difficult client behaviors.
- Evaluate the solution/change, and identify areas for future improvement.
- Study conflict negotiation.
- Engage in consulting self-study via books and other relevant publications.

Beyond technical skills, good consulting requires consulting skills. Whether lending your expertise to work on a project internal to your HR department or collaborating with clients from other departments or stakeholders external to the organization, what will set you apart will be your ability to perform the following effective consultation behaviors:

» Apply creative problem-solving to address business needs and issues.

» Serve as an in-house workforce and people management expert.

» Analyze specific business challenges involving the workforce, and offer solutions based on best practices or research.

» Generate specific organizational interventions (for example, culture change, change management, restructuring, training) to support organizational objectives.

» Develop consultation and coaching skills (that is, entry and contacting, discovery and dialogue, feedback and decision to act, engagement, and implementation, and extension, recycle, or termination).

» Assist business counterparts with thoughtful dialogue about the implications of decisions relative to their impact on other business units or staff in general.

» Guide employees regarding specific career situations.

For example, as an HR professional, you need to be able to understand and discuss a wide range of possible employee benefits; you must be able to state what they are and how they work and detail the differences between them. This is relatively basic and foundational information about benefits. In addition, you must also be able to organize benefits into meaningful categories, compare and contrast, make observations about their use, and perhaps identify patterns within your organization. Beyond your skill in understanding the benefits in your organization and conceptualizing their use, higher-level HR professionals must also be strategic thinkers and, in a way, consultants when it comes to benefits.

Once you have identified patterns and analyzed costs or use, you will need to think strategically about whether you have the right mix of benefits to achieve your goals of attraction or retention of employees. Also necessary will be assessing your data about benefits relative to other data such as turnover or cost projections for offering certain benefits. You then must draw conclusions and formulate a logical argument as to why benefit offerings should be changed—or not changed. And then at the highest level of competency, you will need to extend your thinking and apply concepts clearly across your business so that the approach you take will connect to the strategy of the organization.

Recalling once again our content validation study, we found that *Consultation* is more frequently performed and perceived as more important by senior and executive HR professionals; however, early- and midcareer-level practitioners can acquire the necessary tools, early on, to become effective internal consultants. By developing a proactive perspective on consulting projects, conducting initial investigation of HR-based transactional issues, gathering and analyzing facts and data for business solutions, raising issues and identifying patterns requiring transactional HR solutions, identifying stakeholder needs, providing a summary of pertinent facts and information to midlevel and senior HR leaders, and managing work time efficiently, novice HR professionals can be shaped into successful HR consultants.

For midlevel practitioners, carrying out the following activities will further help develop consultative skills in support of becoming a more experienced HR professional: performing behaviors like evaluating and measuring processes, leading the implementation of business solutions, championing the implementation of strategic initiatives, managing projects within allotted time and budget, coaching direct reports and others throughout the organization using *HR Expertise*, and developing HR and business process improvement solutions.

To work with people and to become a trusted advisor, HR professionals must have solid interpersonal skills. They need to have the ability to put ideas into words, to listen, to give support, to disagree, and to respectfully challenge courses of action to manage relationships. Just like technical skills, interpersonal skills are a necessity to be a successful HR professional and effective internal consultant.

For HR Managers

- Consider having a forum where HR managers and managers from around the organization are used to consult with one another about current organizational challenges and how they may be tackled or better understood.

- Provide opportunities for your team to expand their HR expertise; being an expert in the field provides the foundation for consultation.

- Role play to practice critical consultation skills, as a HR function apply creative problem-solving to address business needs.

- Have less experienced practitioners shadow more experienced professionals during consulting opportunities.

Part IV:
The SHRM Competency Model: Interpersonal Competencies

HR Expertise and *Ethical Practice* cover the most fundamental necessities of HR job performance, and the strategic partner competencies, *Business Acumen, Critical Evaluation,* and *Consultation,* describe the competencies through which HR job performance directly affects organizational outcomes and performance; therefore, it may seem as if we have already covered the entire job of an HR professional. However, just possessing technical knowledge and skill (*HR Expertise*) and applying it in an ethical manner (*Ethical Practice*) to achieve business outcomes (through *Consultation, Critical Evaluation,* and *Business Acumen*) does not translate into HR success. A significant part of an HR professional's job is characterized by interdependence with stakeholders. In other words, the work of an HR professional is largely a function of the need to provide service to other people directly or to address situations and challenges that involve other people. To achieve interdependence with stakeholders, a successful HR professional must develop and maintain interpersonal relationships, share and discuss information, and influence others to achieve common goals. Further, this interaction occurs regularly with people with whom you may not share a similar background, similar perspectives, or even similar working styles. Despite these likely dissimilarities, the successful HR professional must develop productive, enduring working relationships. Such differences between the HR professional and stakeholders or even between HR colleagues leaves a lot of room for potential dysfunction or underperformance as the result of weak interpersonal competence. The successful HR professional is not only technically proficient and acts as an HR strategic partner, but he or she also has interpersonal competence.

The interpersonal competencies are *Relationship Management, Leadership and Navigation, Communication,* and *Global and Cultural Effectiveness. Relationship Management* is the ability to manage interactions to provide service and to support the organization; *Communication* is the ability to effectively exchange information with stakeholders; *Global and Cultural Effectiveness* is the ability to value and consider the perspectives and backgrounds of all parties; and *Leadership and Navigation* is the ability to direct and contribute to initiatives and processes within the organization. Together, this cluster of competencies contributes to HR professionals engaging in smooth business interactions; allows them to foster enduring, productive working relationships with stakeholders and colleagues; and guides them to influence others to achieve common goals.

The interpersonal competencies represent the set of "softer" behavioral competencies that facilitate smooth business interactions and enduring business relationships. Similarly, HR professionals who are proficient in the interpersonal competencies as well as in the other competencies will be viewed as credible, respected business partners to whom stakeholders and colleagues look for support when needed and with whom stakeholders and colleagues enjoy conducting business.

In addition, organizations are increasingly using team-based structures to achieve work.[1] Team success hinges on team member interdependence and interaction, a clear understanding of the work to be done and the development of a path to achieve it, and an integration of a diversity of perspectives. As this phenomenon continues to grow and as organizational structures position team performance, rather than individual performance, as the central focus for organizational success, the interpersonal cluster of competencies will become more central to effective HR performance over time.

Proficiency in the interpersonal competencies is crucial to the long-term success. To understand why this is and how the competencies look operationally, we must take a deeper dive into each of the four competencies.

Chapter 7.

Relationship Management

Relationship Management is defined as the ability to manage interactions to provide service and to support the organization.

HR professionals regularly interact with clients and stakeholders; therefore, job success for the HR professional is largely a function of your ability to maintain productive interpersonal relationships and to help others do the same, or to display competency at *Relationship Management.*

Research has documented positive outcomes associated with productive and healthy interpersonal relationships in the work environment.[1] Positive, formal relationships (for example, an employee's relationship with his or her supervisor) are associated with beneficial outcomes for employees, such as improved feelings of belonging and inclusion in the workplace,[2] increased salary, more promotions, greater career mobility, and other rewards.[3] Positive, informal relationships at work are associated with greater job satisfaction, more involvement, enhanced performance, improved team cohesion, stronger organizational commitment, positive work atmosphere, and lessened intentions to turnover.[4] Employees who have better interpersonal relationships with their co-workers and supervisors may also perceive the organization as more supportive,[5] may be more committed to their organizations, and may experience increased perceptions of fit with their organizations.[6] In sum, healthy interpersonal relationships among employees at an organization contribute positively to an employee's and organization's success.

Let's briefly compare the dynamic of a workforce to that of a sports team. There is no denying that talent is important; softball teams need a pitcher with precision, a successful soccer midfielder has to have stamina, and no hockey team would be able to survive the season without a swift goalie. But possibly more paramount to the success of a sports team—or any team—is cohesion. In the team sports arena, relationships exist among coaches, fans and spectators, captains, owners, managers, mascots, cheerleaders, and others. For teams to "get into the zone"—or to take performance to the next level—they need to enhance team cohesion and deflect any negative rapport. The same is true in the HR world—HR professionals regularly interact with clients, peers, employees, subordinates, supervisors, and stakeholders. Building strong relationships facilitates personal and organizational growth and allows for resolutions to conflicts that are both intrapersonal (within an individual) and interpersonal (within two or more individuals) in nature. For this reason, *Relationship Management* is the first interpersonal competency we will discuss.

Relationship Management, defined as the ability to manage interactions to provide service and to support the organization, encompasses maintaining productive relationships and demonstrating the aptitude to help others to do the same.

The success of HR professionals largely depends on both developing sound working relationships with other people and helping others maintain productive working relationships. In fact, according to our research as well as occupational research reflected on the U.S. Department of Labor's Occupational Information Network (O*NET OnLine),[7] behaviors such as "establishing and maintaining interpersonal relationships" and "resolving conflicts and negotiating with others" are critical to the success of HR professionals (see Appendix B). These findings reflect both the large extent to which HR professionals must interact with other people and

Manage Successful Business Relationships

There are many ways for HR professionals to develop their expertise. Multiple activities should be undertaken continuously over time to develop, maintain, and extend professional expertise. Below are some examples of how to sharpen your relationship management skills.

- Become a mentor or coach/have a mentor or coach.
- Attend networking events to build close relationships with colleagues and clients.
- Become active in external professional organizations.
- Volunteer to work closely with clients, and make yourself available for questions and requests.
- Seek out opportunities to practice active listening techniques and to ask open-ended questions.
- Volunteer to work on a cross-functional project or assignment.
- Work closely with others to develop a new training program or team-building activity.
- Participate in company retreats or team-building activities.
- Assist in conflict management, focusing on an interest-based approach.
- Familiarize yourself with various styles of conflict management.
- Offer empathy and concern when colleagues are in need of support.
- Find opportunities to model a positive attitude, and give colleagues a warm welcome when you interact.
- Seek out opportunities to build trust through honesty and consistency.
- Work to foster a respectful and considerate environment.
- Ask for feedback and input about the effectiveness of your interactions.

their unparalleled position in influencing interpersonal relationships throughout an organization. Individuals performing at the highest levels of proficiency in *Relationship Management* readily:

» Establish credibility in all interactions.
» Treat all stakeholders with respect and dignity.
» Build engaging relationships with all organizational stakeholders through trust, teamwork, and direct communication.
» Demonstrate approachability and openness.
» Ensure alignment within HR when delivering services and information to the organization.
» Provide customer service to organizational stakeholders.
» Promote successful relationships with stakeholders.
» Manage internal and external relationships in ways that promote the best interests of all parties.
» Champion the view that organizational effectiveness benefits all stakeholders.
» Serve as an advocate when appropriate.
» Foster effective team building among stakeholders.
» Demonstrate ability to effectively build a network of contacts at all levels within the HR function and in the community, both internally and externally.

Behaviors for each interpersonal competency will look different depending on the career level of HR professionals—we once again identify shifting proficiency standards. So what do these shifting proficiency standards look like for *Relationship Management*? For an early-career HR professional discovering a conflict among employees, displaying competence would entail providing basic information for resolution of the conflict to all involved parties. At the midcareer level, the HR practitioner may have built on the *Relationship Management* competency such that he or she is able to recognize potential employee relations issues proactively and either resolve the issue or move concerns to senior leaders. At the senior and executive levels, HR professionals would mediate difficult employee relations as neutral parties and then work to create conflict resolution strategies and processes throughout the organization. The focal point of this example is that the *Relationship Management* competency is essential across all career levels; however, what the behavior looks like shifts throughout the duration of an HR professional's career.

Let's explore another example dealing more with relationships among clients or vendors. More junior-level HR professionals (early- and midcareer) demonstrate their *Relationship Management* while serving as front-line liaisons with their organizations' vendors and suppliers and maintaining service quality. Senior-level professionals are responsible for overseeing customer service objectives and outcomes, and executive-level professionals develop and champion organizational customer service strategies and models. The behavioral standards for proficiency in the competency do not entirely alter, but rather they accrue progressively—that is, they accumulate and amplify as an HR professional moves up the career ladder.

If you are looking to build your current *Relationship Management* competency as an HR professional, you can do so by focusing on improving specific behaviors associated with your respective career level. Further, if you are looking to advance in your career, you can review the behavioral standards we have defined by career level and work toward setting goals to meet those standards outlined for advanced levels. In fact, we found through our content validation research that although HR professionals at all career levels rated *Relationship Management* as "important" or "critical" to job success, the importance ratings of this competency steadily increase with career level, and this competency is rated as more important at senior levels (that is, senior and executive) than at junior levels (that is, early and mid).

Essentially, a midcareer-level professional actively aiming to move to a senior-level position can work toward proficiency at senior-level behaviors, such as "providing opportunities for employees to interact and build relationships" and "building consensus and settling disputes internal to HR on policy and practice decisions."

What can you expect to see as you—and, by extension, your organization—build proficiency in this competency? Research highlights numerous positive outcomes as being associated with productive and healthy interpersonal relationships in the work environment:[8]

» Improved feelings of belongingness and inclusion in the workplace.

» Greater job satisfaction.

» Increased performance and involvement by employees.

» More team cohesion.

» Positive work atmosphere.

» Increased organizational commitment.

» Greater sense of organizational support.

Perhaps one of the most significant relationships in an organization is the "leader-follower" relationship, in part because managing good working relationships on its own does not necessarily ensure that actions are aligned to an organization's objectives or desired outcomes. Organizations are continuously turning toward HR professionals to sustain leadership initiatives, and this is one reason why *Leadership and Navigation* (see Chapter 8) is another valuable HR competency.

For HR Managers

- Provide opportunities for HR managers to develop and build relationships across the organization by participating in cross-functional teams—be they in person or virtual.
- Develop formal or informal mentoring programs.
- Encourage your employees to volunteer as a group for team building.
- Demonstrate how to build an effective network of contacts.

Chapter 8.

Leadership and Navigation

HR professionals have been known to "wear many hats"—juggle multiple duties—within their positions. *Leadership and Navigation* recognizes one of the many roles that HR professionals play; this competency addresses those attributes needed by HR professionals to lead organizational initiatives and obtain buy-in from stakeholders. We define the *Leadership and Navigation* competency as the ability to direct and contribute to initiatives and processes within the organization.

Leadership and Navigation is defined as the ability to direct and contribute to initiatives and processes within the organization.

Leadership and Navigation is largely influenced by career level, so proficient behaviors for each career level vary more than with other competencies. Our research suggests that at the early- and midcareer-level positions, *Leadership and Navigation* is not necessarily "required upon entry" into an HR job; however, it is required for HR professionals moving into senior and executive roles. This difference is indicative of developmental opportunities for those junior-level professionals seeking to advance in their careers.

Typical behaviors that effective leaders proficient in *Leadership and Navigation* demonstrate include the following:

» Exhibits behaviors consistent with and conforming to organizational culture.

Lead and Navigate Successfully

There are many ways for HR professionals to develop their expertise. Multiple activities should be undertaken continuously over time to develop, maintain, and extend professional expertise. Below are some examples of how to develop leadership practices.

- Become a mentor or coach.
- Set up a meeting to discuss your professional goals with top-level managers.
- Take the initiative to discuss your ideas, beliefs, values, and opinions in team meetings.
- Create an individual development plan, and work toward completing the appropriate learning experiences.
- Seek out opportunities to create new action plans based on aspirations for the future of the organization.
- Take on additional responsibilities or tasks involved in a job project, even if you feel they will be a bit challenging.
- Attempt innovative approaches to reaching project objectives.
- Attend management training.
- Seek out opportunities to serve as a role model for colleagues.
- Take the initiative to share your expertise on a particular topic.
- Volunteer to be the team leader on a project.
- Assist in the creation and organization of a project team to highlight the strengths of its members.
- Join a leadership board or committee.
- Improve your self-awareness by recognizing your moods and emotions, and their impact on those around you.

» Fosters collaboration.
» Understands the most effective and efficient way to accomplish tasks within the parameters of organizational hierarchy, processes, systems, and policies.

» Develops solutions to overcome potential obstacles to successful implementation of initiatives.

» Demonstrates agility and expertise when leading organizational initiatives or when supporting the initiatives of others.

» Sets the vision for HR initiatives and builds buy-in from internal and external stakeholders.

» Leads the organization through adversity with resilience and tenacity.

» Promotes consensus among organizational stakeholders (for example, employees, business unit leaders, informal leaders) when proposing new initiatives.

» Serves as a transformational leader for the organization by leading change.

We have already emphasized the contribution that the shifting proficiency standards add to each of the competencies in our model, and, in *Leadership and Navigation*, it is paramount to understand how these standards come into play. Because this competency is not as immediately critical for more junior-level professionals, it lends itself to ample developmental opportunities. Professionals should gauge their behavior against the proficiency standards and use the behaviors as a benchmark for what specific actions they should exhibit to progress in their careers.

That is not to say that early- and midcareer-level professionals are unable to demonstrate *Leadership and Navigation* effectively in their current positions. On the contrary, an early-level professional can demonstrate proficiency in this competency by behaving consistently with and representing the culture of the organization and by fostering collaboration with co-workers, and midlevel professionals can manage programs, policies, and procedures to support the culture. For senior-level professionals, behaviors exhibited are a bit more aggressive. They help establish those programs, policies, and procedures that support the organizational culture. At the executive level, professionals lead staff in the HR department to maintain or change the organizational culture as necessary to sustain the business. At each level the behaviors are in support of the organizational culture, but demonstrating proficiency varies by career level. In other words, the competency remains necessary, but the specific nature of the behavior evolves across career levels such that HR executives continue to uphold best practices for the business.

Let's use the Patient Protection and Affordable Care Act to illustrate a specific example of *Leadership and Navigation* proficiency standards, within the SHRM Competency Model, as applied to a real-life challenge. Entry-level HR professionals need to know and understand what the law says and what it means for the health care policies of their organizations, and midlevel HR professionals also need to know how the law is applied to their organizations and if any of their existing policies are in contradiction to the law—or at what point their organizations' policies will no longer be in compliance.

Senior-level professionals must build on this information and strategically think about how they will modify their benefits given the cost implications of their current policies and anticipated direction. They will need to think about use in relation to the demographics of their organizations and to incorporate a knowledge of anticipated trends in health care options, costs, and availability into the resulting shifts in their workforces—growth or retrenchment, for example. And, finally, at an executive level, HR professionals need to be able to present their findings and recommendations in a manner that is consistent with and demonstrates knowledge of their business and the strategic direction that is planned—both in the short and long term.

Conceptualizing Leadership

It may be difficult at times to truly define a leader, as the nature of the position may not always be formal. At its core, *Leadership and Navigation* in the HR profession begins with basic building blocks:

» Listening actively to identify potential challenges or solutions.

» Building credibility with stakeholders.

» Demonstrating flexibility, adaptability, and initiative.

As professionals advance to senior and executive positions, they build on those core behaviors to improve their aptitude for strategizing for the business.

When defining HR leadership, we should note the differences between being a manager of subordinates and being a leader to followers. Perhaps it is easiest to explain these differences with examples (see Table 8.1).

Table 8.1. The Differences Between Managers and Leaders

Managers	Leaders
Actively avoid conflict and work to resolve issues when a conflict does arise	Confront conflict and use it as an asset to drive change improvements
Execute organizational culture strategies	Shape that culture
Communicate business outcomes	Are visionaries for future achievements
Plan the course of action	Set the direction and envision new pathways

Note: Distinguishing these differences is also where we begin to see how Navigation goes hand-in-hand with Leadership.

Traditional Versus Modern Approaches to Leadership

Historically, there have been many approaches to describing leadership. Two worth noting are the trait approach and the behavioral approach.[1] The trait approach focuses on identifying stable characteristics of the leader, such as personality, leadership style, and general skills and abilities.[2] Traits include characteristics such as sociability, empathy, esteem, and ambition. The behavioral approach to leadership examines those specific behaviors associated with effective leadership and team performance.[3] Essentially, researchers observed known effective leaders and attempted to categorize the types of behaviors that those leaders engaged in. Looking at a combination of traits, skills, and behaviors, and aspects of a given situation that moderate the relationship of leader attributes and leadership effectiveness, situational leadership proposes that different attributes will be effective in different situations, and that the same attribute is not optimal in all situations.[4] Given that neither of these approaches fully reveal the likelihood of success as a leader, other theories have surfaced.[5]

Today, we have a considerable number of theories on how one can approach leadership and be an effective leader. One such theory of leadership, transformation leadership, best describes the definition, supporting behaviors, and proficiency standards of the *Leadership and Navigation* competency. Transformational leadership, described by James MacGregor Burns in 1978, and extensively researched by Bernard Bass in the 1990s,[6] suggests that at the essence of good leadership is the attributes for leaders to appeal to followers' deeper motives: justice, morality, peace, and others. Transformational leaders develop a clear vision, change the organization to fit the vision, and motivate employees to reach the vision.[7]

Under the behavioral standards for *Leadership and Navigation*, many of the properties of transformational leadership emerge. Transformational leadership encompasses empowering subordinates— or in this case, early- and midcareer-level professionals—to move beyond working for their self-interests and to work toward a greater cause: a vision for the organization set forth by senior and executive professionals. More advanced leaders transform the junior leaders by reinforcing the value in their tasks and promoting their capabilities. As a result of this process, the subordinates become leaders in the organization as well. These leaders, regardless of career level, are the inspiration behind elevated work performance across the organization.

Motivation in Leadership

Throughout our discussion of *Leadership and Navigation* has been an underlying theme of motivation. This is because one of the most pivotal facets of leadership in HR is attaining the attributes required to instill motivation in others. A modern approach to work motivation includes goal-setting theory, described by Edwin Locke and Gary Latham in 1990.[8] This comprehensive theory describes how setting goals leads to increased motivation in the work environment and, in turn, to higher performance. To summarize, successful individuals set goals that are specific, measureable, attainable, relevant, and time-bound (SMART). Employees who adopt less specific goals—such as "do your best"—are less likely to achieve peak performance. Some studies suggest introducing a feedback loop with your goal setting by making a point to evaluate and readjust your goals—making them SMARTer. In addition to the ability to motivate others, effective leaders themselves need to possess the motivation to lead—meaning leaders, too, should adopt SMART goal-setting practices.

It may come as no surprise that senior- and executive-level HR professionals placed greater importance on *Leadership and Navigation* as being critical to the success of their HR careers. These differences in ratings might be explained by the changing nature of HR jobs across career levels. Early-career professionals are less likely to have leadership responsibilities; instead, HR professionals at more junior levels are often engaged in transactional work. At midlevel, HR practitioners might begin to take on leadership responsibilities, but, even at this level, HR professionals are likely to be continuing to develop their leadership competence on the job or through formal training programs. Not until the senior level are HR professionals expected to have fine-tuned their leadership capabilities, and, at the executive level, leadership is clearly important to the job and a requisite for entry. Overall, these results indicate that the *Leadership and Navigation* competency contributes to HR job performance, albeit differently across career levels, and provides a clear area of development for early- and midcareer professionals who wish to advance into more senior positions.

No matter the career level, the outcomes for an organization with HR professionals proficient in *Leadership and Navigation* are typically positive employee attitudes with regard to organizational commitment and job satisfaction. A true leader understands that organizational goals are not static and that repetitive behavior in a leader may lead to a destructive leadership style. The most effective behaviors a leader can demonstrate revolve around the organizational vision and transformation of behaviors for the good of the organization.

For HR Managers

- Facilitate discussions about the culture and future of the organization, where HR managers can develop their skills of visioning and influencing.
- Include a coaching component in your high potential development program.
- Create high-profile stretch assignments for high potential employees.
- Encourage job rotation.

Chapter 9.
Communication

Effective communication is one of the building blocks of personal and career success.[1] This is particularly true for HR professionals. From fielding employee grievances to collaborating with other organizational units to address business challenges from a human capital perspective, effective communication is essential for describing policies and practices, setting goals, communicating progress, and ultimately realizing an organization's mission and vision. When managers effectively communicate HR practices and policies, employees perceive the organization's HR management (HRM) to be more effective, and, in turn, employee satisfaction and business unit performance are positively affected.[2]

Communication is defined as the ability to effectively exchange with stakeholders, and it is a crucial aspect of many business processes. Though important on its own, *Communication* also supports many of the other competencies, including the other interpersonal competencies (*Relationship Management, Leadership and Navigation*, and *Global and Cultural Effectiveness*).

Communication is defined as the ability to
effectively exchange with stakeholders.

Communication is the foundation on which relationships are built and maintained. Effective communication allows leaders to translate organizational strategies in such a way that other

Communication Developmental Opportunities

There are many ways for HR professionals to develop their expertise. Multiple activities should be undertaken continuously over time to develop, maintain, and extend professional expertise. Below are some examples of how to develop communication skills.

- Participate in training programs to develop your active listening skills and communication fundamentals.
- Pay attention to the communication methods used by senior employees, including your boss or manager; identify which methods are effective or ineffective, and tailor your own communications accordingly.
- Seek out public speaking opportunities.
- Take on an assignment that will culminate in a presentation to a group of stakeholders.
- Take on an assignment that will require communication with stakeholders throughout the process.
- Sign up for a course or workshop to sharpen specific communication skills, such as technical writing, interpersonal communication, or public speaking.
- Carefully prepare e-mail communications—try to be as concise as possible.
- Prepare an agenda for a departmental or organization wide meeting.
- Share a strategic idea in a meeting.
- Develop a training program—communicate to employees why this program will be beneficial.
- Increase your HR-related social media presence.
- Analyze the communications you receive for differences in tone and specificity as directed to different levels and audiences.

employees will easily understand. And the ability to communicate with employees across cultures is a true sign of global and cultural effectiveness. From resolving employee issues to negotiating with stakeholders, communication is key to successful performance as an HR professional.

There are many forms and facets of communication within the workplace. Some of the specific behaviors demonstrated by HR professionals who are proficient at communication include the following:

» Providing clear, concise information to others in verbal, written, electronic, and other communication formats for public and organizational consumption.
» Listening actively and empathetically to the views of others.
» Delivering critical information to all stakeholders.
» Seeking further information to clarify ambiguity.
» Providing constructive feedback effectively.
» Ensuring effective communication throughout the organization.
» Providing thoughtful feedback in appropriate situations.
» Providing proactive communications.
» Demonstrating an understanding of the audience's perspective.
» Treating constructive feedback as a developmental opportunity.
» Welcoming the opportunity to discuss competing points of view.
» Helping others consider new perspectives.
» Leading effective and efficient meetings.
» Helping managers communicate about their business, not just on HR issues they face.
» Using communication technology and social media.

These behaviors can be applied to a variety of settings within the HR profession. For example, you may need to recommend a change in your company's compensation policy. This change will affect a lot of individuals within your organization, so you will need to clearly and concisely communicate your plan and provide relevant information to all stakeholders. Your communications will need to be proactive; rumors may circulate if the correct information is not provided in a timely manner. You will also need to demonstrate an understanding of your audience's perspective by providing unhappy employees with an opportunity to share competing opinions and by listening actively and empathetically to their differing points of view. Perhaps you can help them consider the policy from a new perspective, by competently communicating its benefits and taking into account their constructive feedback.

Combining these behaviors provides an overarching picture of communication in the life of an HR professional, which can be applied to many different platforms, situations, and audiences.

All of these behaviors were rated as "important" or "critical" to effective job performance by HR professionals, and it is likely that you will find a use for many, if not all, of them during your HR career. When you consider the integral role that communication plays every day on the job, it will come as no surprise that 90 percent of our content validation study participants indicated that *Communication* is "required upon entry" into any HR position. This number remains essentially consistent across organizations ranging in size from fewer than 100 employees to 25,000 individuals. The percentage of HR professionals rating *Communication* as "required upon entry" is also consistent across organizational sectors.

Though communication skills are necessary for HR professionals at all career levels, you have time to advance your skills as your career progresses. The behaviors related to communication also change as you move from one career level to the next. For example, an early-level HR professional needs to be able to clearly communicate issues to notify upper management of concerns, whereas an HR executive would be more likely to communicate strategic messages to employees across the organization.

These differences in proficiency standards, which are dependent on career level, demonstrate the wide reach of the *Communication* competency and are indicative of the developmental opportunities available during your career progression. For example, early-level HR professionals may want to focus on producing accurate and error-free communications, on communicating policies and procedures, and on using discretion when communicating sensitive information. In contrast, midlevel HR professionals may want to hone their skills at delivering presentations, translating organizational strategies, listening actively to understand stakeholder concerns, and delivering constructive feedback. At the senior levels, you may begin to create channels for open communication across and within levels of responsibility, to engage in conversations with stakeholders, and to oversee culture communication strategies. Finally, as an executive, you may find that setting communication goals, such as articulating alignment between HR initiatives and organizational strategies and communicating the corporate mission and vision to other stakeholders, will move to the forefront.

Most, if not all, aspects of an HR professional's job involve some form of communication, and therefore, proficiency in *Communication* can have a strong positive impact within an HR department, as well as within an organization as a whole. In addition to its contribution to various business activities, clear and concise communication regarding HR practices and policies is viewed positively by employees and can result in increased employee satisfaction and business unit performance.[3] Unclear communication can also be problematic for teams spread across different workplace locations.[4] As diverse and global teams become more common, it is more crucial for HR professionals to stay on the cusp of communication trends and continue to improve and enhance their skills to maintain team and organizational cohesion.

Communication allows the HR professional to be influential—or not—in driving strategic discussions. The best HR initiatives, unless communicated well, will not be implemented or fully provide the return on investment that is possible. Technical HR expertise may not prevail without the support of behavioral competence in communication.

For HR Managers

- Critique communications as a way of building expertise in creating clear and effective communication.
- Provide opportunities to write, either formally or informally, through industry publications and/or social media.
- Encourage public speaking and in-house presentations.
- Practice effective closed-loop communication.

Chapter 10.
Global and Cultural Effectiveness

As the workforce becomes increasingly global and diverse, HR professionals must have the ability to work with employees from diverse backgrounds. *Global and Cultural Effectiveness* is defined as the ability to value and consider the perspectives and backgrounds of all parties. As an HR professional, you may find yourself at the forefront of diversity initiatives, such as diversity training, in which case you should know how to interact with employees from various cultures to successfully facilitate these programs. HR practitioners also need to be aware of various laws and regulations in hiring practices to ensure organizational compliance and to take steps to promote and maintain a diverse workforce.

Global and Cultural Effectiveness is defined as the ability to value and consider the perspectives and backgrounds of all parties.

You may protest that *Global and Cultural Effectiveness* does not apply to you or your organization if you work within a single country and your organization does not have a global presence. However, *Global and Cultural Effectiveness* does not apply only to international companies or to international assignments. Regardless of location, your company should employ individuals from a variety of backgrounds, and as an HR professional, you must be able to effectively interact and maintain productive working

Developing Global and Cultural Competence

There are many ways for HR professionals to develop their expertise. Multiple activities should be undertaken continuously over time to develop, maintain, and extend professional expertise. Below are some examples of how to develop global and cultural awareness.

- Participate in global conference calls or Skype interviews to experience global differences.
- If feasible, accompany another staff member on a global trip.
- Become the mentor or buddy of an expatriate HR manager.
- Take on the assignment to learn and understand the variety of cultures that are currently present in your organization.
- Participate in employee relations scenarios in which cultural differences appear to be at least part of the underlying problem.
- Collaborate with colleagues from different generations on a work project.
- Host multicultural team-building opportunities.
- Assist with preparing an employee for an expatriate assignment.
- Identify what inclusion might look like in your organization or how it might be different from location to location.
- Develop a draft training program related to inclusion and awareness, and then work with staff to revise the program—thereby learning or being exposed to new perspectives.

relationships. *Global and Cultural Effectiveness* encompasses many types of diversity, and HR professionals who are proficient in this competency will find that they are able to "appreciate the commonalities, values, and individual uniqueness of *all* human beings," not just of those who are similar to themselves.[1] Overall, HR professionals who are proficient at *Global and Cultural Effectiveness*:

» Have a strong set of core values while operating with adaptability to particular conditions, situations, and people.

» Maintain openness to others' ideas and make decisions based on experience, data, facts, and reasoned judgment.

» Demonstrate nonjudgmental respect for other perspectives.

» Work effectively with diverse cultures and populations.

» Conduct business with an understanding and respect for the differences in rules, customs, laws, regulations, and business operations between their own culture and all cultures.

» Appreciate the commonalities, values, and individual uniqueness of all human beings.

» Possess self-awareness and humility to learn from others.

» Embrace inclusion.

» Adapt perspective and behavior to meet the cultural context.

» Navigate the differences between commonly accepted practice and law when conducting business in other nations.

» Operate with a global, open mindset while being sensitive to local cultural issues and needs.

» Operate with a fundamental trust in other human beings.

» Take the responsibility to teach others about the differences and benefits that multiple cultures bring to the organization to ensure inclusion.

» Incorporate global business and economic trends into business decisions.

For example, *Global and Cultural Effectiveness* can be applied on the job when you are implementing, revising, or evaluating diversity training within your organization. During this process you will need to work effectively with individuals from diverse cultures and populations. Whether your organization is domestic or international, it will be your responsibility to teach others about the differences and benefits that multiple cultures bring to the organization. During this process, you will most likely seek input from individuals of diverse cultures within the organization. You will need to maintain openness to their ideas and demonstrate nonjudgmental respect for their perspectives. If the diversity training initiative will be implemented across global locations, you will need to be sensitive to local cultural issues and needs and demonstrate an understanding and respect differences in rules, customs, laws, regulations, and business operations between your own culture and those of the global locations.

Though many of these actions and behaviors apply across career levels, *Global and Cultural Effectiveness* does not always manifest in the same way, and some behaviors may be more pertinent to junior and senior career professionals. For HR professionals early in their careers, possessing general knowledge of local culture, respecting differences, promoting inclusion, and demonstrating a willingness to develop and grow their understanding of this competency will serve them well. Midlevel HR professionals should be prepared to put this knowledge and willpower to work, implementing and auditing organizational and HR practices to ensure global/cultural sensitivity; designing, recommending, or implementing diversity/culture programs; and employing cultural sensitivity in communicating with staff. Moving on to the senior level will involve developing policies that are consistent and fair to members of all backgrounds, creating diversity and cultural enhancement programs, and providing mentoring/training on cultural trends and practices to all levels of the organization. Finally, at the executive level, HR professionals should maintain expert global and cultural knowledge/experience and apply this knowledge by integrating perspectives on cultural differences and their impact on the success of the organization, proving the return on investment of a diverse workforce, and using a global economic outlook to determine the impact on the organization's human capital strategy.

Practicing behaviors such as those described above will enhance your *Global and Cultural Effectiveness* and allow you to lead by example, whether you are working in an organization with locations throughout the world, an organization based solely in the United States, or any combination thereof. The cultural flexibility and tolerance for ambiguity encompassed within *Global and Cultural Effectiveness* are especially important for those working across countries, with individuals from a variety of cultures. Individuals from various countries have been acclimated to different cultures and cultural practices. Therefore, the lenses through which they view the world vary, and these variations influence the ways they communicate and interact in the workplace. HR professionals who are proficient in *Global and Cultural Effectiveness* maintain knowledge about these differences and are able to apply this knowledge throughout all aspects of HR management. These characteristics of a diverse workforce are useful to consider within HR processes such as training, performance management, and feedback delivery, as well as within recruitment and selection in international settings.

Cross-cultural experiences outside of work, such as traveling to other countries and interacting with individuals from various cultures, can also help to positively influence your cultural flexibility and effectiveness. HR professionals who are proficient in *Global and Cultural Effectiveness* should always seek to understand the perspectives of others and to incorporate these perspectives into business decisions and processes. After all, diverse teams are often able to come up with new and creative ideas and solutions to problems that might not have otherwise been explored. Overall, as stated earlier, HR professionals should seek to "appreciate the commonalities, values, and individual uniqueness of all human beings" in any and every way that they can to enhance their personal growth and success, as well as that of the organization.[2]

For HR Managers

- Interact one-on-one with individuals who are new to the organization or who need to be included in a project in the organization—particularly if they are coming from outside the current location or represent a very different perspective.
- Celebrate diversity.
- Discuss the importance of heterogeneous teams and practice what you preach.
- Take the opportunity to incorporate global business and economic trends into business discussions.

Part V:
Building Your Road Map

The SHRM Competency Model is an integral part of your career development. The model will help you find your place in the field of HR, understand where you want to go, and determine how you will get there.

Of course, not all HR professionals have a clear picture of where they are, let alone where they want to be. That is only natural. Look how much the business world has changed in recent years. The United States has witnessed the acceleration of a shift from a manufacturing economy to a knowledge economy. Many U.S.-based organizations have outsourced labor. The business environment has become increasingly global.

Organizations themselves have changed. Middle management has been squeezed out of many companies. Organizations have turned to flexible teams, mergers and acquisitions, and innovative technology, all of which have led to upheaval in some industries.

And HR has changed. For example, who foresaw the transformative impact of social media on recruiting? Meanwhile, the push to make HR more strategic has succeeded unevenly, but transactional HR is definitely not the future of the profession. HR leaders need to earn their seat at the table every day by understanding the business and by providing business solutions through human capital.

Despite all these changes and uncertainty, developing skills in HR basics will never go out of style. Nor will learning how best to apply these behaviors that we described in the SHRM Competency

Model. But these skills and behaviors need to be learned proactively through a well-thought-out journey.

If you have only an approximate understanding of where you are in your career and where you are going, you might wander around, wasting your time and energy and the time and energy of your employer. You might stumble across your destination, but it is unlikely. And you might not even recognize it if you found it.

Thinking about an uncertain future can be overwhelming. Using the SHRM Competency Model, you can employ three basic steps to help you plan for your professional development.

Find Yourself on the Map

The first step is to figure out where you are in your career. You cannot determine how to get somewhere without understanding your starting point. Even if you have a vague idea of where you are, you need to determine the exact coordinates.

Being honest is important. There are no advantages to pretending to be father along your career path than is actually the case; such a misstep could get in the way of real progress. Remember: No one starts off knowing everything he or she needs to know about HR. In fact, no one finishes his or her career knowing it all.

Determine Where You Want to Go

The second step is to figure out your destination. What are your career objectives? Setting your goals is a highly personalized process, but you have to develop a clear understanding of what you are aiming for.

Your destination might change somewhat over time, but as long as you have an idea of where you want to go, you can find the resources that will help you make course corrections as conditions change.

Make a Plan to Get There

The third step is to create a road map for achieving your career objectives. Once you know where you are and where you are trying to go, you need to figure out the path you will take.

What is the exact path? What resources and experiences will you need to get there? At what points throughout your journey will you need these? What are the milestones along the way? How do you handle career setbacks? How do you handle life events that delay or threaten your progress? And how do you know when you "arrive"?

In the chapters that follow we will explain each of these steps in more detail. We encourage you to set aside some time to think about and create your road map.

Consider how essential global positioning system (GPS) devices have become in our lives. In our cars and smartphones, they can pinpoint our location within a few feet. In addition, software shows us the various streets and geographic features in our neighborhood. If you have identified a specific destination, the GPS device can give you turn-by-turn directions to get there.

Chapter 11.
Your HR Career Path

Career planning involves the development of a career path or road map that individuals use to guide their career advancement. These road maps are created, in part, by examining alternative career options, making decisions that might affect your current career, and planning for career progression from one level to the next.

This is not a single, narrow path. You will be developing multiple competencies at various stages and through various means as you use the road map to advance. Think of a three-dimensional topographic map; then add the additional dimension of time. The result is a rich, intuitive, valuable tool.

Career planning involves the three steps we mentioned earlier: find yourself on the map, determine where you want to go, and make a plan to get there. Let's look at them in more detail.

Step 1: Find Yourself on the Map by Conducting a Self-Evaluation

You need to understand where you are in your career. You might have a fairly good idea, yet as you go through the process, you might find some surprises. Perhaps in a previous job—or even in a previous career—you developed some skills or demonstrated certain behaviors that put you a little farther along than you realize. Or maybe an aspect of your skills, such as in posting job openings, might be less advanced than your title would suggest.

How do you determine where you actually stand on each of the SHRM competencies (or any other HR-related competencies)? Accurately assessing your own competencies will allow you to identify your training and development needs, build a long-term career path, and understand what you need to do to reach the next level of your career.

Whether you are looking for someone to rate your own competencies or you are working to set up a competency initiative in your HR department, you should first consider who will provide competency ratings. Competency ratings can be made by a variety of sources. Included are self-ratings, supervisor ratings, peer ratings, or even ratings from objective sources such as a test. Each rating source has both benefits and drawbacks that should be carefully considered, and there is not a one-size-fits-all approach. Instead, you should think about how the ratings will be used (for example, for identifying self-development needs or for performance management) and then make a determination regarding who will make them.

Each rating source provides one piece of the overall puzzle when understanding your strengths and developmental opportunities within each of your competencies. We have depicted the ratings sources in Figure 11.1. Looking at this figure, each rating source provides a set of information (the light gray bubbles), and these bubbles overlap to some degree—the overlap between these bubbles reflects the overlapping information provided by these rating sources. However, the figure also shows that these ratings do not overlap entirely—that is, each one provides specific information, in addition to the information that is common to other rating sources.

Self-Ratings

Self-ratings, as the name implies, are ratings made by you about yourself. Although not without limitations, self-ratings have several benefits. First, they can provide information that might be difficult

Figure 11.1. Rating Sources

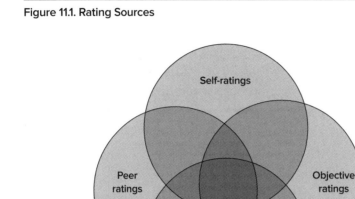

for others to observe. For example, you are likely the best person, rather than a co-worker or supervisor, to describe your own thought process when dealing with an ethical dilemma. Second, when used for purposes such as performance appraisal, self-ratings can provide employees with the sense that they have input into performance ratings that are made by others (such as supervisors). Third, comparing ratings you made about yourself with ratings that someone else (for example, peers or supervisors) made about you can be an enlightening experience that increases self-awareness. We discuss this aspect more below in the section on 360-degree assessments.

Supervisor Ratings

Possibly the most frequently used source of competency ratings is supervisors. Supervisors are in a unique position to provide ratings because they are often most familiar with the day-to-day work of employees and their strengths and limitations as they pertain to the position. In many organizations, supervisors are also responsible for performance appraisals—this responsibility often gives supervisors an in-depth understanding of what employee behavior is valued by the organization. Additionally, because supervisors are tasked with translating organizational goals and directives into actionable items for employees, they understand the performance goals that meet organizational needs. For these reasons, as well as for the general prevalence of supervisor ratings for administrative purposes (for example, performance appraisals, determining raises and promotions) in organizations, supervisors are an excellent source of competency proficiency ratings.

Co-Worker Ratings

Competency ratings can also be made by your co-workers. A primary advantage of co-worker ratings is that in many organizations employees work in team settings. Because of the frequent interactions that most people have with their co-workers, these ratings are a valuable source of information that can supplement self or supervisor ratings. However, co-worker ratings are often lower than self and supervisory ratings for a variety of reasons. In some organizations, co-workers may be in competition with one another for rewards (for example, performance bonuses, and promotions). Co-workers may also lack the competencies and experience needed to make accurate ratings. Although co-worker ratings are extremely useful as an additional source of information for identifying training or development needs, co-worker ratings should never be used for administrative purposes, such as performance appraisals.

Using Multiple Sources

As we alluded to in Figure 11.1, combining rating sources can provide the most comprehensive information. The reason is that different rating sources come from different perspectives, and how employees view themselves is likely to differ from the views of co-workers and supervisors. Each rating source provides distinct information, and when used together these sources provide a picture that takes into account multiple perspectives. Additionally, significant insight can be obtained by understanding how ratings differ from one another. For example, examining how and why self-ratings vary from those made by peers or supervisors may be valuable.

One multirater assessment, known as a 360-degree assessment, has become common over the last decade In short, 360-degree assessments obtain ratings from multiple sources, including supervisors, peers, customers, and subordinates. We provide a graphic example of the 360-degree assessment in Figure 11.2. In fact, a huge benefit of these assessments is their multisource nature—as we mentioned above, multisource feedback is beneficial for obtaining the full picture when rating competencies.

Figure 11.2. 360-Degree Assessments

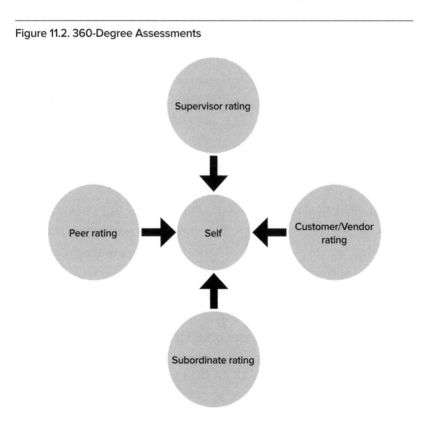

After you have a solid understanding of the types of ratings you can use to assess your proficiency on each of the nine competencies in the SHRM Competency Model, you will be ready to start your development journey. HR careers can develop and advance at different levels in the various competencies over time; no one has mastered it all. Do not be too concerned if you are strong in a few competencies but lack accomplishments in others. That is the nature of HR—and the nature of any career.

In fact, it is not uncommon for an HR professional to be at a midcareer or senior level in certain competencies, for example, *HR Expertise* or *Communication,* and to be at a lower level in other competencies, such as *Critical Evaluation* or *Ethical Practice.*

As we discussed, you should talk to colleagues, supervisors, and others who know you well to acquire meaningful information about your proficiency in each of the competencies. Or more formally, you might want to solicit the input of former bosses and colleagues and even non-HR people in your organization and outside of it. The purpose is to gain an accurate picture of where you are, not to impress anyone.

Let's take the *Consultation* competency as an example. Based on the work that you have been assigned, you might have had the opportunity to manage a sizable project, including its vision, design, implementation, and evaluation. Perhaps this project helped you come up with a strategic HR and business solution that was communicated to senior staff. This accomplishment would indicate an executive-level proficiency standard.

But perhaps the nature of your HR department and your work assignments has not provided you with the opportunity to work closely with line managers regarding HR practices. That would put you at an early-career level of proficiency in that portion of the *Consultation* competency.

Factors such as organization size, HR department size, industry, career level, and even the way your supervisor allocates work can have an impact on your proficiency levels within the nine competencies. Again, there is no shame in lacking experience in certain facets of HR. This task is merely a fact-finding exercise.

These facts will help inform and shape your choices in the next step.

Step 2: Determine Where You Want to Go, and Set a Vision for Your HR Career

Where do you want your HR career to be in three or five years? How about 10 years, or 20, or more? If you have not thought about it, now is the time.

Maybe you want to be the director of an HR department, or the chief human resource officer of a corporation. Perhaps you see yourself as a benefits specialist or labor relations expert for a decade or two. There is no right or wrong choice—there is only the best choice for you.

Though you probably cannot expect your vision of 20 or more years from now to be realized exactly, it is good to be aspirational and to periodically revisit your long-term goals. Your career will change, and your life will change.

Start by assessing your career interests. What do you really like to do? What are you best at? Often, these are the same—but not always. Some people have a natural talent for communication but would rather not be responsible for explaining benefits or writing a newsletter. Others find deep satisfaction when given the chance to lead a team but are rarely given that opportunity in their current jobs or organizations.

What are your core values and needs? Are you a people person? Are you drawn to nonprofit organizations because of their mission or because you have a desire to serve the public? Do you like hands-on work or prefer to delegate? Is financial security paramount for you? Your family and friends?

This is a good time to stake stock of your personal life and personal goals. You do not want to have these and your career clash, if you can avoid it. Will you be raising children, traveling extensively, or caring for aging parents? What is your vision of your work/life balance, now and down the road?

As you set your vision, do not assume that you will or will not stay at one organization throughout your career; this could delay or limit your progress. Remember, this is about you and your career, not just about your current job or boss or employer.

Once you have asked yourself these questions, evaluate the results with a mix of realism and aspiration. Knowing where you are in your career is valuable, but you should not be limited by your starting point. Where you go—what you want to do with your career—is something that only you can decide. Take the advice of everyone you can talk to, but do not be afraid to dream big.

Step 3: Make a Plan to Accomplish Your Career Goals

Start by studying the difference between where you are now and where you want to be. This gap identifies your areas for development. You will be seeking out informal and formal opportunities to advance your career. They will help you with your current position and future jobs as well.

An exercise that you performed as part of your self-assessment was determining where you stand on the proficiency standards for the nine competencies. Now, you can take those data and determine where you want to grow. Which competencies are most important to you? Which behaviors are the ones that you most want to develop? Which specific proficiency standards that you do not currently meet are the ones that you wish to reach?

Next, you will determine specific actions to take to reach the proficiency standards you have identified. This will take some time. You will need to consider a wide range of resources, which are discussed later in this chapter. But when you have completed this task, you will have created your personal career path—the key to success in your HR career.

This career path will be unique to your situation. And it will be revised as situations and career and life changes occur. Think of it as your personal GPS system recalibrating your course or being updated with new software as new roads and destinations are created.

Developing Your Individual Career Path

Career paths are significant because they allow you to visualize your future and determine the steps necessary to reach your goals (see Figure 11.3). They provide you with the opportunity to develop behaviors within each competency, and these behaviors and competencies act as stepping stones in career development. Taking twists and turns overtime, career paths can include many forms of career progression.

Figure 11.3. Career Path Opportunities

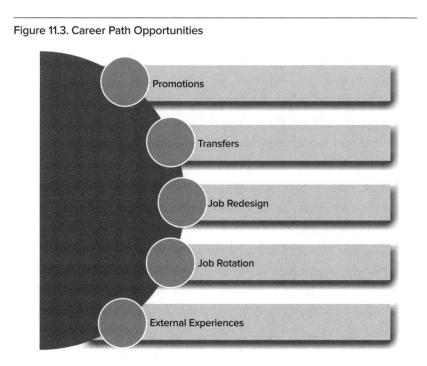

Your HR career path may be vertical. This path involves upward movements, or promotions, within an organization, also known as "climbing the ladder." For instance, you may progress from a supporting role in your early career, to a managerial role during midcareer, to a directorial role as a senior HR professional, and finally to an executive role. This progression requires the development of certain competencies and skills, which will be discussed later in this chapter.

Or you may have the opportunity to progress horizontally within an organization. *Horizontal career paths* involve lateral movements, or *transfers*, within an organization; employees stay at the same rung of the ladder, but they are able to broaden their skills and experience new challenges by taking on different work roles.

Other career path opportunities involve embarking on a less traditional journey. These experiences may replace traditional paths, or they may be combined with traditional paths as developmental opportunities prior to advancement.

For example, there may be opportunity to *redesign your current position* providing additional or alternative challenges and opportunities within your current job. This path provides you with the opportunity to learn new skills and develop existing skills; it is often used to prepare for future opportunities. Job redesign may include enlargement (adding new challenges and responsibilities) and enrichment (increasing the depth of current job responsibilities).

Another less traditional opportunity is *job rotation*, which involves the systematic movement from job to job to provide a varied perspective and to broaden your expertise. Job rotation is often used by managers to gain experience as they prepare to progress to the next level of their careers. It may also be used by early-career professionals who want to gain a wide variety of experiences prior to choosing a specialization.

Finally, *external experiences*, such as consulting and contingent work, may be valuable opportunities for you to develop your skills using a route that is more flexible than traditional career paths.

These positions typically do not offer traditional advancement opportunities, but they are created to provide you with the opportunity to work with a variety of organizations and potentially in a variety of roles. As you develop your path, take the opportunity to inquire with your supervisor or mentor about the possiblility of job redesign, rotation, or performing consulting work.

Career paths should be developed through collaboration between you and your manager or mentor. Managers and mentors should encourage you and provide you with feedback, support, and guidance. Discussions should revolve around career interests, strengths and weaknesses, and developmental plans.

During the career path development process, managers or mentors should discuss your career goals and evaluate your readiness for development and progression. You and your managers or mentor should also discuss the results of competency assessments; as we have discussed, these evaluations can be used to assess strengths and weaknesses and serve as a foundation for development. Demonstrated competencies can be compared to competencies required for future positions to determine gaps that need to be filled prior to progression.

Once competencies have been evaluated and gaps have been identified, a career path can be developed including developmental activities to fill the gaps and career progression opportunities based on current and future skills. At this point, managers or mentors can communicate career opportunities within the organization that will suit your chosen path and skill set.

Along with types of career paths you should consider what pace they progress at. For some, a slow but steady career progression may be preferable, due to its allowance for work/life balance and other outside interests. For others, a fast route, including rapidly increasing responsibility and growth, will better suit their career aspirations. Regardless of the type of path or pace, you should partake in developmental opportunities to continually progress along your chosen path (see Figure 11.4).

Figure 11.4. Competency Assessment to Career Path Development Process

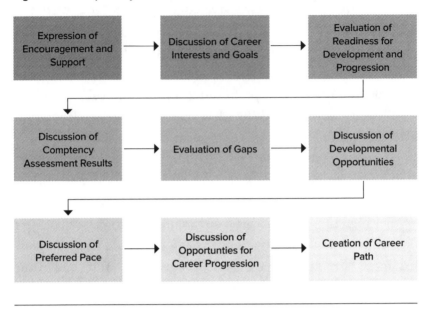

Employee Development

Like career paths themselves, opportunities for you to develop may take many forms. For some, formal education may provide a needed career boost. For others, targeted job experiences based on competency assessments may be all that are needed to progress along their path.

A variety of methods for you to development are detailed below. Overall, development choices should be based strategically on your career path; developmental opportunities should help you fill the gaps identified during career path creation and master the competencies needed for the next career step.

Competency assessments play a leading role in your development across career paths. To progress to new or different roles, HR professionals need to expand their HR-specific knowledge, skills, and abilities.

Formal Education

Formal education can help you develop the skills you need to progress further in your career. Many colleges and universities offer master's degrees in HR management. HR professionals may also consider a master of business administration (MBA) with a concentration in HR. Though certainly not required for progression, advanced degrees can open doors to new opportunities and provide you with many of the skills you need to compete for more challenging positions and projects.

Professional Certifications

Professional certifications allow you to demonstrate a level of HR mastery based on standardized professional content and may serve as a worthwhile step toward career progression. Various certifications are available—including the SHRM Certified Professional (SHRM-CP) and the SHRM Senior Certified Professional (SHRM-SCP) that use as their foundation the SHRM Competency Model—focusing on different knowledge, skills, and behaviors required within the profession.

In addition to a competency-based HR certification, there are other relevant certifications in areas such as compensation, benefits, project management, and so forth that may be valuable for HR practitioners to consider, depending upon the role or career aspirations one possesses.

Job Experiences

Job experiences are the most common form of development. New projects, responsibilities, and relationships serve as learning experiences every day. You should be encouraged, or ask for the opportunity, to develop new skills and knowledge by taking on a challenging project outside your comfort zone or taking the time to get to know employees whom you have not worked with previously. Additionally, opportunities that are often incorporated into career paths (such as transfers, job redesign, and job rotation) can provide useful knowledge, skills, and abilities needed for opportunities farther along the path (such as promotions). Like other forms of development, job experiences should be tailored based on your goals and the opportunities available within your organization.

Interpersonal Relationships

Similar to job experiences, interpersonal relationships allow you to learn and grow every day on the job. However, specific relationships, such as those with a mentor or career coach, may be particularly useful for targeted employee development, and as previously mentioned, mentors or career coaches are good sources for helping you identify opportunities for development.

A mentor is a more experienced employee who helps a less experienced employee learn and grow. Mentoring relationships can develop informally, based on shared interests, or formally, through a company effort to foster organizational mentoring and development. Mentoring relationships can be beneficial for both the mentor and the protégé. The protégé receives career support, exposure, and visibility, as well as psychosocial support from a positive role model. Meanwhile, the mentor is given the opportunity to develop his or her interpersonal skills and demonstrate worth to the organization.

Career coaches typically serve as a more formal resource for employee development (see Figure 11.5). Career coaches may provide feedback to employees based on competency assessments or interviews with co-workers and managers in a personalized one-on-one fashion.

Figure 11.5. Competency Development Opportunities

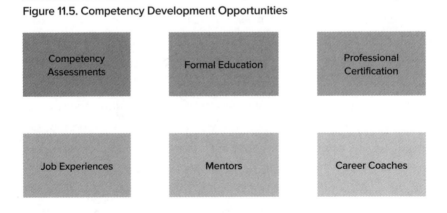

They help identify and provide employees with resources, such as subject matter experts, courses, and job experiences, that will help them develop. Coaches are often used to develop high-potential employees who are being groomed for management positions. They are usually external professionals hired by the employee or by the organization to support employee growth.

Setting Challenging Yet Attainable Goals

In addition to identifying your competency strengths and weaknesses and the developmental opportunities that best meet your needs, you will want to establish multiple goals along your career path progression—one goal for 30 years out will not suffice. And achieving most of the goals will mean that it is time to set some more.

Exclude goals that are not attainable. Select those that are achievable and challenging and that can really drive home your success. Your career path should be based on goal-setting theory (see Figure 11.6).

Recall our previous discussion in Chapter 8 of professors Edwin Locke and Gary Latham's research on goal-setting theory, which posits that specific and difficult goals are correlated with higher performance than are vague goals[1], and that to motivate employees, goals must have clarity, challenge, commitment, feedback, and task complexity. You should begin to evaluate developmental opportunities and activities using these goal-setting techniques, targeting at least a few of the competencies, and seek out training and other activities that link to these competencies.

Consider timing your development. Certain competencies will be more important, and their behaviors more attainable, early in your career. Others will be more relevant in your peak years. Some might take decades to master.

Understand that the SHRM competencies overlap and intersect in many ways. For example, communication skills boost effective consultation performance. Skills from several competencies serve to improve employee relations efforts.

Figure 11.6

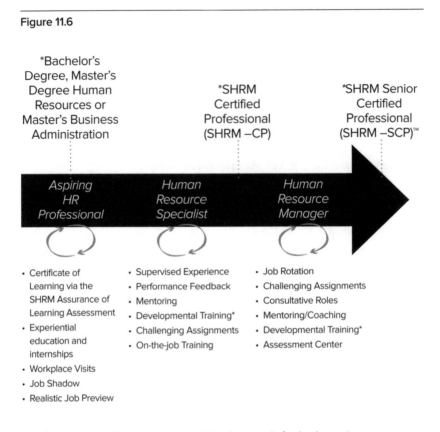

*Bachelor's Degree, Master's Degree Human Resources or Master's Business Administration

*SHRM Certified Professional (SHRM –CP)

*SHRM Senior Certified Professional (SHRM –SCP)™

Aspiring HR Professional

Human Resource Specialist

Human Resource Manager

- Certificate of Learning via the SHRM Assurance of Learning Assessment
- Experiential education and internships
- Workplace Visits
- Job Shadow
- Realistic Job Preview

- Supervised Experience
- Performance Feedback
- Mentoring
- Developmental Training*
- Challenging Assignments
- On-the-job Training

- Job Rotation
- Challenging Assignments
- Consultative Roles
- Mentoring/Coaching
- Developmental Training*
- Assessment Center

SHRM HR Diagnostic Tools™ measure strength and opportunity for development.

Professor Wayne F. Cascio of the University of Colorado said: Competencies contribute to individual exemplary performance and create a reasonable impact on business outcomes. For us to really appreciate where we can contribute, we need to know the business inside and out. That's going to play into the development of so many of these competencies. Communication, relationship management, consultation: They're not independent.[2]

Most professionals should strive for proficiency in the behavior standards in each of the nine competencies for their respective career levels. Reaching proficiency in your core functional area, meaning the knowledge that you need to develop for your current job role or function, is more crucial. Often, these skills are found in the *HR Expertise* competency.

HR Expertise covers a lot of ground. Its subcompetencies include strategic business management, workforce planning, compensation and benefits, risk management, employee and labor relations, HR development, technology, global capabilities, talent management, and change management. You will not be able to become highly proficient in all these areas, but you can choose the ones that are most valuable to you and your supervisor.

If you are a generalist, you should have substantial knowledge in each of the areas. If you are a specialist, you should still have some knowledge in each of the areas, but it would probably be much more specialized and targeted in one area. For example, a compensation and benefits specialist would have deep knowledge in this area but still have familiarity with other functions within *HR Expertise.*

In addition, you can develop proficiency in the portions of the eight behavioral competencies that are most significant for your career.

One of the strong points of the competency model is that you can be proficient at varying levels within behavioral competencies at various times within your career. So, for example, you can focus on increasing your proficiency within *Relationship Management* in the near term. As you grow in your career, you might want to become more proficient in the related aspects of *Business Acumen or Leadership and Navigation.*

You do not have to focus on the competencies in which you are weakest. You may decide to put your initial emphasis on competencies that allow you room for development and that help guide you to where you want to go.

Our content validation research demonstrates that all the competencies are important to all HR professionals. All nine competencies are relevant regardless of your role, regardless of the size of your organization, regardless of your function. However, you should weigh their importance to you based on your situation and your career aspirations.

It might not be clear initially that a competency is applicable to your position. For example, you might think that *Ethical Practice* is irrelevant to benefits administration—until you discover that a manager is trying to ignore overtime laws or you encounter a claim of falsified time cards.

Another example: A labor relations specialist dealing with unionized workforces will need to become an expert in how to deal with practices such as salting and with a plethora of laws that apply to unionized workforces. But he or she cannot ignore the other competencies.

The way you translate your labor relations knowledge into success is by engaging in consultation behaviors, relationship management behaviors, and communication. You will use the eight behavioral competencies to maximize the positive impact of your knowledge.

Chapter 12.

Finding the Resources You Need

What resources can you use to assess your current proficiency?

You can rely on a variety of resources available from SHRM, from your employer, and from many other places. Try to think as broadly as possible, and investigate all options.

The first area to consider is that of assessment. How will you come up with a clear, detailed picture of where you stand in terms of the skills and behaviors you have mastered and those that you have yet to master?

As you know, you can gain valuable input from your colleagues, your immediate supervisor, others in your organization, and other people who know you and are familiar with your work. Former bosses and colleagues can also help. Non-HR people—particularly managers with whom you have worked—might have valuable insights.

You may conduct an informal or a more formal competency assessment. If you chose to assess your competency proficiency less formally, as you go through the competency model and examine the lists of essential behaviors and the associated proficiency levels, circle the ones you are unsure about. Then, ask various people whether they believe that you have demonstrated the ability to use that behavior consistently and effectively. For example, if you are measuring your progress in the *Leadership and Navigation* competency and believe that being adept at "leading change" is important to your career, ask trusted advisors to tell you honestly whether you have demonstrated a proficiency level such as the midlevel standard of "serves as manager of organizational initiatives within units" or even the senior-level standard of "serves as a change agent for the organization."[1]

In addition, you should consider talking to professionals who are at a similar stage in their HR careers or who hold a position that will be of interest to you soon or farther down the road. Learn how they got there. Walk through the competency model with them, and ask about the best ways to develop in the identified areas.

The collection of input you receive from all these assessments will serve as the baseline for determining in which areas you want to improve.

If you choose to assess your competency proficiency more formally, SHRM has created a suite of diagnostic tools to help meet your needs. The SHRM Diagnostic—*Self Tool* empowers you to identify opportunities for development and target ongoing personal and career growth activities.[2] Created for HR professionals, these tools create momentum: from assessment, to development, to achievement.

The self-diagnostic tool will assess your competencies, identify areas of existing strength, and uncover opportunities for development. The SHRM Diagnostic—*Self Tool* is relevant across all HR career levels and organization sizes and sectors and is applicable in a global context.

Following the identification of your strengths and opportunities for development, you need to find the resources for developing your career. These are the momentous turns, routes, and destinations that make up your personal road map to HR success.

Again, SHRM will be a great source. Seminars and workshops—including some offered online—will help. Some will be targeted for your level or desired level of accomplishment. In addition, look for local opportunities that may be targeted at the business community or environment in which you work—these could be industry-specific or through state or local laws.

SHRM conferences are also valuable. You can attend a conference whose theme aligns closely with your current or planned area of expertise—such as talent management or diversity and inclusion. And you can attend the Annual Conference & Exposition, for which you can map out a track of sessions dealing with your area of interest, such as *Business Acumen* or *HR Expertise.*

Ask your employer what educational and developmental offerings it can provide. Some might be offered in-house; others might be external but still available at little or no cost to you.

Competency-based certification through SHRM can be a terrific way to gauge your accomplishments and add to your skills and abilities. And you might decide to purse a college-level course or other training on your own time and your own dime.

Regardless of which resources you choose, it would be valuable to talk to your supervisor, mentor, or both about creating a personal development plan based on your competency needs assessment. Even if your organization does not provide training or developmental opportunities immediately, the conversation will demonstrate your commitment to improvement and might yield opportunities the next time that your manager reviews his or her training budget.

Chapter 13.
How Does Certification Fit In?

With his groundbreaking research in 1973, David McClelland posed a serious question—should we be assessing competencies rather than general intelligence?[1] The question has long since been debated by educational measurement and testing professionals alike with the aim of establishing the best predictor of competence and performance.[2]

In the realm of certification, this same question has been bandied about for nearly 40 years.[3] This debate has been no more intense than in recent years when numerous professional societies and associations have gone beyond the assessment of technical knowledge to assess the application of knowledge. One such example of this movement is the American Institute of Certified Public Accountants (AICPA). During the early 1990s and 2000s, AICPA shifted its testing model from one of job knowledge (that is, testing knowledge of generally accepted accounting practices) to one of job knowledge and ability (that is, testing knowledge of generally accepted accounting practices and the ability to apply them to a practical exercise). Other examples of this shift include the National Board for Professional Teaching Standards (NBPTS) and the American Society of Association Executives (ASAE). In more recent times, other professional societies such as the Accreditation Council for Graduate Medical Education (ACGME) and the Association of American Medical Colleges (AAMC) have started the transition to competency-based assessment. Each of these examples represents the need to assess more than knowledge because of the possibility for ensuring greater productivity and reducing potential error among professionals.

Despite a clear movement to competency-based assessment and certification, there is a stunning lack of consensus on the best approach to assessing competencies. In some cases like NBPTS and ACGME, interviews, work samples, and portfolios are used to assess proficiency, whereas in other cases like AICPA, a practical exercise with role play might be used to assess effectiveness as an accountant. With others like AAMC, situational judgment tests serve as the best model for assessing proficiency in communication, teamwork, and bedside manner. Although research suggests that each of these approaches serves as a valid means of discriminating between proficient candidates and those lacking proficiency, it is clear that approaches are selected based on viability and the audience needs.

With factors like the stewardship of the HR profession in mind, SHRM has undertaken the daunting task of building a better certification model—a competency-based certification model. Leveraging its extensive research in HR competencies, SHRM now offers the gold standard for HR professional certification—the SHRM Certified Professional (SHRM-CP) and the SHRM Senior Certified Professional (SHRM-SCP).

SHRM and Certification

HR professionals worldwide look to SHRM for comprehensive resources to help them function effectively at their jobs, develop their careers, and partner strategically with employers. SHRM also works to advance the HR profession as a whole, ensuring that as business evolves, HR evolves to meet business needs. Increasingly, business understands that effective people management is a strategic imperative. As a result, employers expect that HR professionals will demonstrate, in addition to having a thorough knowledge of HR concepts and requirements, the behavioral competencies required to effectively *apply* that knowledge in the modern workplace in support of organizational goals.

The SHRM Competency Model is fundamental to SHRM's two new certifications, the SHRM-CP for early-career practitioners, and the SHRM-SCP for senior-level practitioners. SHRM is launching these new credentials to further two goals: for HR professionals, to reaffirm the importance of acquiring both the competencies and knowledge essential for successful job performance, and for employers, to provide reliable indictors of proficiency in these critical dual aspects of modern HR practice. SHRM regards the SHRM-CP and SHRM-SCP as the new standards in certification for the HR profession. By incorporating key HR competencies into the SHRM-CP and SHRM-SCP, SHRM has increased the relevance of the new certifications.

SHRM's new credentials demonstrate to the global business community that the credential holder has strong capabilities in both aspects of HR practice—competency and knowledge—that are required for effective job performance. The SHRM Body of Competency and Knowledge (SHRM BoCK), summarized in Figure 13.1, also draws heavily on the SHRM Competency Model. The SHRM BoCK documents the HR behavioral competencies and functional areas of knowledge areas tested on the SHRM-CP and SHRM-SCP certification exams. The SHRM BoCK is also the common framework for item writers developing questions and for individuals developing exam preparation materials. SHRM operates exam development and study material development as separate, independent functions, and observes a strict firewall between these activities to protect the integrity and credibility of the certification exams.

The SHRM-CP and SHRM-SCP test an HR professional's knowledge and his or her ability to translate that knowledge into business outcomes by leveraging these core competencies. Although the behavioral competencies represent the bulk of the competencies, *HR Expertise* comprises several functional knowledge domains.

Human resource management (HRM) functions can be grouped into numerous frameworks. A common strategy for grouping HR functions is through the lifecycle approach in which each function is tied to specific stages of the employee lifecycle from beginning to end. Other models focus on the transactions carried out by professionals. Our research indicates a more effective means for categorizing HR functions is to take a stakeholder perspective. Key segments of HRM can be grouped into one of three stakeholder perspectives: people, organizations, and the global workplace. In addition, every part of HRM is bolstered by effective business leadership and strategy. Figure 13.1 represents the knowledge domains covered in the SHRM BoCK.

Figure 13.1

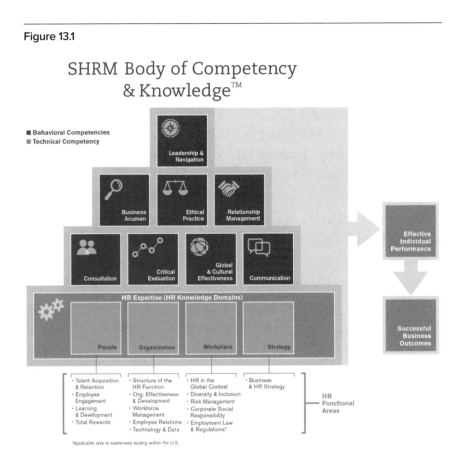

SHRM Body of Competency & Knowledge™

The SHRM BoCK is the content basis for both certification examinations. All concepts tested by these examinations are represented in this body of knowledge. The SHRM BoCK outlines core functional responsibilities for the HR profession. In addition, it highlights the relevant knowledge areas and competencies needed for successful practice in these functions. The SHRM BoCK was developed using a rigorous job analysis involving more than 35,000 HR professionals and business leaders worldwide (this number includes research participants from the development of our competency model and the content and criterion-related validity research that supports it). The knowledge areas and competencies were validated for relevance using subject matter experts from business and academia. The validity of these knowledge areas and competencies was further established by conducting a large-scale, multiorganization criterion validation study with more than 2,000 HR professionals and their supervisors.

Developing SHRM Certifications

SHRM conducted a three-part knowledge specification exercise to develop the SHRM BoCK component identifying the main areas of HR functional knowledge or *HR Expertise*, the single technical competency in the SHRM Competency Model (see Figure 13.2). First, SHRM performed an extensive review of the existing literature on HR knowledge, including textbooks, curricula, syllabi, and other educator resources, to determine the universe of potential knowledge areas needed by HR professionals. SHRM also consulted academic and employer surveys regarding the basic functional knowledge needed for participation in the human resource field. SHRM drew on this research to create a preliminary knowledge framework for the SHRM-CP and SHRM-SCP certifications. SHRM then established a BoCK Advisory Panel to validate this framework. This panel included 19 HR and business leaders from various industries, including retail, research, consulting, health care, and manufacturing. The panel reviewed the proposed framework for HR technical knowledge for accuracy and comprehensiveness; defined responsibility statements and knowledge topic areas associated with each knowledge domain and functional area; and developed importance rankings and weights for each knowledge domain. After completing these tasks, a panel subgroup further refined the framework by incorporating additional panel feedback. Upon completion, SHRM adopted the framework as the basis for the knowledge component of the SHRM BoCK.

Figure 13.2. Developing the SHRM BoCK

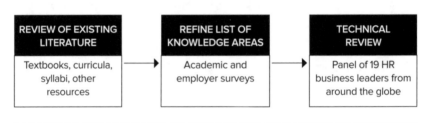

REVIEW OF EXISTING LITERATURE	REFINE LIST OF KNOWLEDGE AREAS	TECHNICAL REVIEW
Textbooks, curricula, syllabi, other resources	Academic and employer surveys	Panel of 19 HR business leaders from around the globe

The foundation for the SHRM BoCK is the notion that effectiveness as an HR professional is a function of two things: (a) knowledge acquired and (b) the ability to apply that knowledge through key behaviors. Together, these technical and behavioral competencies lead to success as a practitioner of HR management. Because technical and behavioral competencies are vital to the practice of HR, all competencies needed to practice HR must be delineated.

Exam Overview

The SHRM-CP and SHRM-SCP exams are based on the SHRM BoCK and its two major aspects of modern HR practice, competencies and knowledge. Accordingly, the exams contain two types of questions:

» Knowledge items, which cover the four knowledge domains

(people, organization, workplace, and strategy) associated with the SHRM BoCK's Technical Knowledge competency.

» Situational judgment items, which cover the knowledge, skills, and abilities (KSAs) associated with the SHRM BoCK's behavioral competencies.

Knowledge items assess candidates' understanding of factual information. Examinees are asked questions in particular subject areas. Situational judgment items assess candidates' KSAs and decision-making skills, which are not easily measured using traditional knowledge-based questions. Examinees are presented with realistic work-related scenarios and asked to choose the best of several possible strategies to resolve or address them.

The field test items on the SHRM-CP or SHRM-SCP exams will be interspersed randomly in the exams so that candidates will not be able to identify them. Examinees' answers to field test questions will not count toward any part of their final exam scores. Field testing gathers data on a question's effectiveness before it can be included on future exams as a scored item. This process facilitates SHRM's efforts to continuously assess and improve all aspects of its certification program. Table 13.1 provides an overview of the score weighting for the SHRM-CP and SHRM-SCP exams.

SHRM-CP and SHRM-SCP At a Glance

- The SHRM-CP exam contains 160 items: 130 scored questions (90 knowledge items and 40 situational judgment items) and up to 30 unscored field test questions.
- The SHRM-SCP exam contains 180 items: 150 scored questions (90 knowledge items and 60 situational judgment items) and up to 30 unscored field test questions.

HR professionals worldwide benefit from certification. Certification provides an acknowledgment of proficiency attained over the course of one's education and career. To date, the HR

Table 13.1. Score Weighting for Test Domains

Domain	SHRM-CP (160 items)	SHRM-SCP (180 items)
People	20%	10%
Organization	20%	10%
Workplace	15%	10%
Strategy	10%	20%
Competencies	35%	50%

profession has relied on knowledge-based certification models to demonstrate proficiency and value to business. As with other professions, a revolution in HR certification has begun with the goal of demonstrating value and proficiency by certifying based on knowledge *and* competencies. As the chief steward of the HR profession, SHRM now offers the gold standard in HR professional certifications, the SHRM-CP and SHRM-SCP. These new credentials further demonstrate SHRM's commitment to advancing the HR profession and to serving the HR professional.[4]

Chapter 14.

How Can You Benefit from the SHRM Competency Model?

We asked a number of people to talk about how the SHRM Competency Model can help build an HR career—and how some are already using the model. The commenters ranged from veteran thought leaders to young people starting out in the field.[1]

Wayne F. Cascio, Distinguished University Professor and the Robert H. Reynolds Chair in Global Leadership at the University of Colorado-Denver School of Business, had this to say about the SHRM Competency Model:

> These competencies are aspirational. Probably there's no single person in the field who embodies all of it. Everybody's going to have some individual strengths, and then in other areas, not necessarily weaknesses, but they're not really your strong suit, and you can still be very successful in the field. You might have someone who's brilliant at data analysis but not as effective in relationship management or leadership and navigation.
>
> There are many paths to success in this field. It's unrealistic to expect that any single person would embody all nine of these competencies, but they are extremely valuable kinds of skills to strive for.

J. Jane Cohen, SPHR, is senior vice president of human resources for Volunteers of America, a faith-based service organization established in 1896 and now employing 16,000 people, including about 100 HR professionals. "The SHRM competencies resonate with me. I really grew up in HR, starting as an HR administrative clerk and going through a lot of different career steps. I can see how the behaviors apply at different levels.

"I've been trying to make HR a higher-level profession within the organization. The model is a great tool." She said that the SHRM Competency Model "applies very closely to the public sector" as well as to the private sector.

"The Competency Model is key for every HR professional," said Craig Southern, Ph.D. (ABD), SHRM-SCP, PHR, IPMA-CP, HCS, SWP, and director of human resources and risk management for Georgia's State Road & Tollway Authority. "I always look for tools to help me with my career and performance."

He agreed with Cohen that the SHRM Competency Model applies to the public and private sectors equally.

"HR is HR, no matter where you go. The only differences I ever see are in the ability to make decisions—on occasion, if there is a governing body outside of the organization." For example, he said, the state legislature might intervene in a pay issue.

May Han, a life insurance industry HR expert who most recently was an HR project manager in Taiwan, is translating the SHRM Competency Model into Chinese to help her colleagues grow in addition to furthering her own career. She said she is using the model "to check which level I am at, and I will chose the proper competency I am interested in to go further. The model helps me see expected HR behaviors and pushes me to know the skills I should equip myself with if I need to go deep in HR waters.

"This model and content help me to know the concrete behaviors in each competency and by different level. This can help my colleagues learn if they want to move to an upper level or to different area. So, it is a good HR career self-measure and development tool or map," said Han.

"As this document was created by so many experts from

different countries, it offers a global level benchmark for local or regional HR practitioners," she added.

Shari Benson, SHRM-SCP, SPHR, is vice president and human resources manager at LERETA, LLC, a tax service firm, in Covina, California. "We do it all here. There are four in our HR department, and 350 employees" serving a multisite and multistate company.

She said that by using the SHRM Competency Model, she identified strategy and workforce planning as areas that she needed to work on. She said she likes online courses and has signed up for three based on the model: strategic partners, HR integration with the business, and workforce planning and staffing.

"As for knowing her company's business: I don't need to know it intimately. But I need to know it better than I do." She said that when she first encountered it, "I thought that the model was something that could help me to grow further. I could go do it and see: Where do I fall? . . . It was great. I was able to determine that I do this fairly well and that there are things that I can do better."

Mia Frankel, SHRM-CP, PHR, an HR specialist at Femme Comp Inc., a U.S. Department of Defense contractor in the Washington, D.C., area, was hired as an HR assistant out of college. At first, she was supporting projects. After four years on the job, she is leading those projects. And she is taking on more responsibilities, such as employee benefits.

About her first encounter with the SHRM Competency Model, she said "I knew what competencies were. But I had never thought about what was needed in HR.

"At the time, I was transitioning to a midlevel professional. We dissected each area," she noted. "I made check marks next to entry-level and midlevel responsibilities I had done and areas I was strong in, and I made check marks on areas I needed to work on."

For example, she discovered that "I ranked low on ethical practice. In technical experience, I was doing very well. In some areas in which you are weak, it might be that you have no experience in that realm" rather than what you do is substandard, she said.

"Sometimes I feel that my experiences are a drop in the bucket; there's so much to know. It's almost overwhelming. I realize that there are a lot of areas that I have made progress in and that there are some areas in which I need to do some work," said Frankel. One year after starting to use the model to guide her development, "I definitely have hit more check marks as I make the transition to mid-career level."

Will she continue to use the competency model?

"Absolutely. I've kept my notes on file as I have used it. I revisit them at the time of my appraisal, and I incorporate them into my goals as well. I'm trying to improve my awareness of new laws and regulations and trends that affect HR. I'm a SHRM member, and I read *HR Magazine*. I'm always looking for webinars I can learn from."

Chapter 15.

Never Stop Learning

There is so much to know in HR that it seems like you can never catch up. As this book went to press, some of the key issues of the day were privacy, intellectual property, skills gaps, Baby Boom retirements, generational conflicts, and, of course, health care. Keeping up with all the legal and regulatory developments can be exhausting, despite all the resources you can call on—not the least of which are the news products SHRM offers on its website, in *HR Magazine*, and in many other venues.

But beyond these specific issues, there are skills and behaviors to master that leverage basic knowledge, as this book has revealed. Knowing the business of your organization, defining your role, mapping your future—it all takes time and energy. There is always the danger of burnout in HR, as in any profession. But one lesson remains constant: You should never stop learning.

That learning might be informal—the kind you gain from a mentor or through the challenge of leading your first employee workshop. It might be formal, such as attending a seminar or securing an HR certification or advanced degree.

As you map out your path to HR success and build your career, we hope that you will frequently refer to the SHRM Competency Model. Even though SHRM will update it as needed, the model remains flexible and enduring: Behaviors will not change much; it is how you apply them that will vary.

We have found through our research that individual HR

professionals who improve their skills and exhibit effective behaviors boost not only their careers but also the performance of their organizations. In the process, they can achieve a third positive result: improving the HR profession. In fact, some thought leaders suggest that HR professionals have an obligation to build the profession.

We hope that this model will encourage HR professionals to think of themselves as more than just a transactional, tactical, day-to-day, I've-got-to-keep-the-trains-running kind of person. We hope they see that all of those tasks are important but that they fit into a larger picture, and that as an HR professional, you are and should be bound to understand what the bigger picture is and how what you do contributes to the bigger picture. We also hope the model will be useful to those who manage other HR professionals as a guide for selection and as a developmental tool for influencing how HR professionals learn, grow, and develop.

The competency model should encourage HR professionals to think of themselves as HR practitioners and also to consider how they fit within the whole HR sphere, and how others around them fit within the HR sphere. And they should contemplate how the HR profession is viewed by others outside HR.

HR needs to evaluate both the risk of doing something and the risk of not doing something. In other words, be forward-thinking and ask: What is the risk of me not engaging in this behavior or taking this risk? What is the risk of having somebody else be the leader in this area?

Some say the future of this profession will come far less from compliance issues and much more with recognizing that we are all really in the business of managing risks.

Many HR professionals are striving to be well rounded, knowledgeable, and competent in all areas of human resources—always striving to do better, whatever they can, to be all they need to be. To get there:

» Roughly 1.3 million people use SHRM resources for professional practice and purpose.

» More than 35,000 HR professionals have served as contributors to the development and validation of the SHRM Competency Model.

» Tens of thousands are now SHRM-CP and SHRM-SCP certified using this competency model, with thousands more per day.

All of these indicators demonstrate the profession's commitment to continuous improvement.

Competency-based talent management makes a difference.

Has it made a difference for you?

Appendix A:
SHRM Research Spotlight: Developing HR Professionals

Professional Development & Succession

Does your organization:

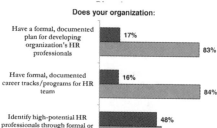

Have a formal, documented plan for developing organization's HR professionals — 17% / 83%

Have formal, documented career tracks/programs for HR team — 16% / 84%

Identify high-potential HR professionals through formal or informal succession planning — 48% / 52%

Note: n=638-682. Respondents who indicated "Don't know" were excluded from this analysis.

HR Competency Models

Has your organization adopted or developed an HR competency model?

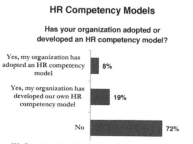

Yes, my organization has adopted an HR competency model — 8%

Yes, my organization has developed our own HR competency model — 19%

No — 72%

Note: n=589. Respondents who indicated "Don't know" were excluded from this analysis.
Percentages do not total 100% due to rounding.

Key Findings

Do organizations have formal, documented plans for developing HR professionals? About the same proportion of organizations have a formal, documented plan for developing their HR professionals (17%) as having formal, documented career tracks/programs for their HR team (16%).

Are organizations identifying high-potential HR professionals through succession planning? Nearly one-half (48%) of organizations identify high-potential HR professionals through succession planning.

What percentage of organizations have adopted or developed an HR competency model? Overall, 27% of organizations have either adopted or developed their own HR competency model. Larger organizations (25,000 or more employees) are more likely to have an HR competency model than smaller organizations (1-24,999 employees).

What competencies distinguish the top HR role from the role directly below the top position? The top HR professionals reported these top three competency areas: strategic management (54%), mentoring HR employees (35%) and relationship management (35%).

What professional experiences best prepared top HR professionals for their role? The top three responses were: work experience (70%), education and professional development (50%), and holding leadership positions (33%).

In your current role as the top HR professional (or among those at the top) in your organization, what competency areas clearly distinguish your role from roles at the level directly below your position?

Top HR Professional

Competency	%
Strategic Management	54%
Mentoring HR Employees	35%
Relationship Management	35%
Knowledge & Experience	34%
Decision Making	25%

Note: n = 458. Percentages do not total 100% due to multiple responses.

In your current role as an HR professional directly reporting to the top HR executive in your organization, what competency areas do you believe clearly distinguish the top HR executive role from roles at the level directly below the top position?

One Level Below Top HR Professional

Competency	%
Strategic Management	66%
Relationship Management	42%
Knowledge & Experience	27%
Business Acumen	23%
Influence	23%

Note: n = 83. Percentages do not total 100% due to multiple responses.

What professional experiences best prepared you for your role as the top HR professional in your organization?

Top HR Professional

Experience	%
Work Experience	70%
Education & Professional Development	50%
Held Leadership Positions	33%
Breadth/Variety of Experiences	28%
Mentoring and Shadowing	18%

Note: n = 433. Percentages do not total 100% due to multiple responses.

What professional experiences do you believe could best prepare you for the role as the top HR professional in your organization?

One Level Below Top HR Professional

Experience	%
Work Experience	63%
Participation in High-level Functions & Decision Making	45%
Education & Professional Development	36%
Taking on Additional Responsibility	29%
Networking & Relationships	26%

Note: n = 76. Percentages do not total 100% due to multiple responses.

Methodology | A sample of HR professionals was randomly selected from SHRM's membership database, which included approximately 250,000 individual members at the time the survey was conducted. Overall, 1,297 responses were received, yielding a response rate of 11%. The margin of error is +/- 3%. Data were collected July 29-August 19, 2011.

© November 2011 Society for Human Resource Management

Appendix B:
Content Validation Study of the SHRM Competency Model

Content Validation Study

OF THE

SHRM COMPETENCY MODEL

Contents

Executive Summary

In keeping with SHRM's mission of serving and advancing the human resource (HR) profession, SHRM developed the SHRM Competency Model. This model comprises nine competencies that describe the attributes needed for successful performance as an HR professional. The model is intended to be applicable to all HR professionals regardless of personal characteristics such as job function or career level and regardless of organizational characteristics such as organization size, work sector and location. These features make the SHRM Competency Model applicable as a guide for the entire HR profession.

Development Steps for the SHRM Competency Model

An extensive review of the professional and academic literature was undertaken to identify existing models and best practices.

More than 100 focus groups were conducted with HR professionals around the world to gather input about the content of the model.

A content validity survey of more than 32,000 HR professionals was completed to confirm the content of the model. Respondents rated the importance of each competency and its requirement upon entry into an HR job, and demographic and organizational characteristics were collected to investigate subgroup differences in ratings.

Results of the Content Validation Survey

All the competencies were rated as important or critical to the success of HR professionals, and all the competencies were rated as required upon entry into an HR job by a majority of respondents. A summary of these findings can be found in the Appendix.

The model's key behaviors were all rated as important or critical for job success.

Although the competencies were rated as important or critical to job success regardless of career level, they are especially important for more senior-level HR professionals. A similar pattern of results was also found for the required-upon-entry ratings, indicating that more senior-level HR professionals are expected to be well developed in each of these competencies. This finding likely reflects the increase in responsibility at more senior career levels, including the expansion of managerial responsibilities and a move from more transactional to more strategic job responsibilities. These career level differences provide a clear developmental path for early-career HR professionals who wish to advance their careers.

Only minimal differences in ratings were found across organizational sizes and work sectors. These relatively invariant results speak to the universal nature of the model.

Summary

These findings provide strong evidence for the applicability of the competency model to the HR profession.

Early-career and mid-level HR professionals need to develop their competencies to be successful at more senior levels of the organization.

Data from more than 32,000 HR professionals provide strong support for the content validity of the SHRM Competency Model and its applicability to the entire HR profession.

Introduction

As a global leader in service to the human resource (HR) profession, the Society for Human Resource Management (SHRM) is committed to empowering HR professionals with the proper tools and resources needed to succeed. With more than 275,000 members in over 160 countries, SHRM recognizes that successful HR professionals use both expertise and experience to carry out organizational strategy and to achieve organizational goals. To accomplish these duties, HR professionals must develop and use their technical and behavioral competencies.

In keeping with SHRM's mission of serving and advancing the HR profession, and in response to member feedback requesting a resource that addresses the work of HR professionals across all career levels, SHRM set out to identify the competencies needed to succeed as an HR professional. Through extensive research across the globe, SHRM created a comprehensive competency model, the SHRM Competency Model. This model encompasses nine competencies, one technical and eight behavioral, and proficiency in these competencies provides the basis for effective performance as an HR professional.

This report describes the content validity evidence for the SHRM Competency Model. In the following sections, this report first provides an overview of competencies and the SHRM Competency Model, as well as an overview of the HR career levels built into this model. Second, this report describes the methodology used to investigate the content validity of the model, including an overview of the survey approach, participants and content (i.e., survey materials). Third, the results of the content validation survey are described and summarized for each competency. Results are also provided for key behaviors and for each competency by career level, organization size and work sector. Last, these findings are summarized.

What Are Competencies?

A competency refers to a cluster of knowledge, skills, abilities and other characteristics (KSAOs) needed for effective job performance. A set of competencies that define the requirements for effective performance in a specific job, profession or organization are collectively referred to as a competency model (Campion, Fink, Ruggeberg, Carr, Phillips, & Odman, 2011; Shippmann et al., 2000).

Competencies can be either technical or behavioral. Technical competencies primarily reflect the knowledge-based requirements of a specific job category (e.g., HR professionals). In the SHRM Competency Model, the technical competency is *Human Resource Expertise (HR Knowledge)*. The other eight competencies in the SHRM competency model are behavioral, reflecting the application of knowledge from the *Human Resource Expertise* competency. Behavioral competencies are more general and at surface level can apply across multiple job categories. Behavioral competencies describe the specific and observable behavior associated with effective job performance and reflect the ways in which knowledge is applied. Although the general concepts associated with the behavioral competencies are not specific to HR (e.g., *Communication*), the content of those competencies is specific to the HR profession, especially when paired with the HR-specific technical competency *Human Resource Expertise*.

SHRM Competency Model

The SHRM Competency Model comprises nine competencies that HR professionals need for success across four HR career levels. For each competency, the model provides a definition of the competency, related subcompetencies, key behaviors and proficiency standards. The SHRM Competency Model is graphically depicted in Figure 1, below.

Subcompetencies are small clusters of KSAOs embedded within each of the nine competencies. Subcompetencies are not distinct from the core competency. Rather, they are more specific manifestations of the general competency they are a part of. In aggregate, the subcompetencies form each competency.

Key behaviors are the behaviors associated with each competency that the most competent HR professionals engage in while performing their jobs. These behaviors contribute to an expanded, broad operational definition of each competency. They are narrower and more specific than subcompetencies.

Proficiency standards are specific, job-relevant behaviors associated with performance on each competency at each of the four career levels. As proficiency standards are specific to each career level, a unique set of proficiency standards exists for each career level for each competency.

Development of SHRM's Competency Model

To develop the competencies and the overall model, SHRM followed best practices, as delineated by the Society for Industrial and Organizational Psychology (SIOP) taskforce on competency modeling, as well as by relevant academic and professional literature about competency modeling (e.g., Campion et al., 2011; Shippmann et al., 2000). Based on a review and synthesis of relevant research and professional literature, SHRM first developed a working model to describe the competencies needed by HR professionals. This review focused primarily on existing HR competency models as well as on literature that describes the work responsibilities of HR professionals. To refine the model, SHRM staff trained in industrial-organizational (I/O) psychology and then conducted 111 focus groups in 29 cities across the globe. This process captured input from over 1,200 HR professionals. During these focus groups, participants edited, revised and enhanced the working model to ensure that it accurately reflected the attributes of successful HR professionals.

Figure 1.1. SHRM Competency Model

HR Career Levels

SHRM has identified four career levels for HR professionals: early career, mid, senior and executive. Table 1.1 provides a general description of the four career levels. These career levels reflect the varying types of responsibilities for which HR professionals are accountable. Specifically, earlier career levels (i.e., early career and mid level) reflect responsibilities that are more transactional in nature, whereas more senior career levels (i.e., senior and executive levels) reflect responsibilities that are more strategic in nature. These career levels were created to reflect the fact that the job of HR professionals differs qualitatively across career levels, a concept incorporated into and reflected in the SHRM Competency Model.

Table 1.1. HR Professional Career Levels and Descriptions

Career Level	Typical Characteristics
Early	• Is a specialist in a specific support function, or is a generalist with limited experience. • Holds a formal title such as HR assistant, junior recruiter or benefits clerk.
Mid	• Is a generalist or a senior specialist. • Manages projects or programs. • Holds a formal title such as HR manager, generalist or senior specialist.
Senior	• Is a very experienced generalist or specialist. • Holds a formal title such as senior manager, director or principal.
Executive	• Typically is one of the most senior leaders in HR. • Holds the top HR job in the organization or a VP role.

Content Validation Study

The purpose of the content validation study was to empirically investigate the accuracy and relevance of the content of the SHRM Competency Model for describing the attributes needed by successful HR professionals. Content validation is a necessary, but not sufficient, step to ensure that the model accurately reflects the requirements of the HR profession. Although the model was developed through an extensive review of the literature and based on the input of subject matter experts (SMEs), this content validation study provided additional quantitative data about the content of the model from a large sample of HR professionals.

Content validity evidence can be collected by asking SMEs to provide ratings (e.g., importance, relevance) of the model's content (Campion et al., 2011). The advantage of a large-scale, quantitative approach is that the data can identify information in the model that is inaccurate, irrelevant or not important. Additionally, the extensive data collected through a large-scale survey allow for differences across demographic and organizational characteristics to be evaluated.

Procedure

On February 8, 2012, SHRM launched the Content Validation Survey. The survey was open through February 24, 2012. To complete the survey, participants were first asked to identify the HR career level that most closely described their own career level. Throughout the remainder of this report, this self-identified career level is referred to as "identified career level." Survey participants then provided importance and required-upon-entry ratings for each competency and aspirational behavior—these ratings are detailed in the "Measures" section of this report. Importantly, survey respondents were asked to rate competencies or behaviors only for their career level—for example, mid-level HR professionals provided ratings only with regard to the model for mid-level HR professionals. Last, participants completed personal and organizational demographic information.

Participants

The survey was sent to the majority of SHRM's professional membership. SHRM members who were not HR professionals, such as members employed primarily in academia, were excluded from the study. In total, roughly 210,000 survey invitations were sent, and 32,314 members responded to the survey, representing approximately a 15% response rate.

Participant demographics are presented in Table 1.2. A majority of respondents (73.4%) were either mid- or senior-level HR professionals with between 11 and 25 years of experience as an HR professional (51.5%). Respondents worked across a variety of organization sizes (as measured in number of full-time equivalents, or FTEs), and worked primarily in for-profit organizations (70.5%). Although some demographic categories contained only a small percentage of respondents, the large sample size of this survey still allows for confidence in the results for these subgroups. For example, although only 4.1% of respondents identified themselves as early-career professionals, the total sample size for this subgroup is still quite large, representing approximately 1,325 HR professionals.

Table 1.2. Participant Demographics

Category	% of Participants
Career Level	
Early	4.1
Mid	32.6
Senior	40.8
Executive	22.5
Years as an HR Professional	
<1 year	.8
1-5 years	10.9
6-10 years	21.6
11-25 years	51.5
>25+	15.2
Organization Size in Full-Time Equivalents (FTEs)	
1-99	26.9
100-499	38.3
500-2,499	21.6
2,500-24,999	11.1
25,000+	1.9
Organization's Work Sector	
Publicly owned for-profit	24.7
Privately owned for-profit	45.8
Nonprofit	17.5
Government	8.3
Other	3.6

Note: Due to rounding, totals may not add up to 100%.

Between model development and model content validation, the resulting model reflects input from HR professionals from 33 nationalities. The list of nationalities represented in the model development and content validation process is presented in Figure 1.2.

Figure 1.2. Nations Represented in Model Development and Content Validation

Australia	India	Scotland
Bahamas	Ireland	South Africa
Bahrain	Israel	South Korea
Brazil	Malaysia	Spain
Canada	Mexico	Thailand
China	Myanmar	Turkey
Dominican Republic	Nigeria	Uganda
Egypt	Pakistan	United Arab Emirates
Germany	Portugal	United Kingdom
Ghana	Qatar	United States of
Haiti	Saudi Arabia	America
		Vietnam

Measures

Each participant rated both competencies and key behaviors. These ratings are detailed in this section. Rating scales are provided in Table 1.3 and Table 1.4, and are described below.

Importance Ratings: Competencies and Key Behaviors

Participants rated the importance of each competency for an HR professional to successfully perform his or her job at the identified career level. This rating was made for all nine competencies. Participants also rated the importance of key behaviors for an HR professional to successfully perform his or her job at the identified career level. Participants provided these ratings for every aspirational behavior for each competency.

Table 1.3. Competency and Competency Behavior Importance Rating Scale

Importance Ratings	
How important is this competency or aspirational behavior to effective job performance for HR jobs at the <identified career level> level?	
Rating	**Response Scale Anchors**
0	**Not Important** The competency behavior/competency is *not required* to perform HR jobs effectively, and it *could not* result in any consequences on overall effectiveness.
1	**Minor Importance** The competency behavior/competency has *minor* impact on effective HR job performance. Without this competency behavior/competency, HR professionals could *generally still perform* these jobs effectively, and it could result in *relatively minor impact* on overall effectiveness.
2	**Important** The competency behavior/competency has an *important* impact on effective HR job performance. Without this competency behavior/competency, HR professionals *would have difficulty performing* these jobs effectively, and it could result in consequences on overall effectiveness.
3	**Critical** The competency behavior/competency has *critical* impact on effective HR job performance. Without this competency behavior/competency, HR professionals *could not perform* these jobs at even a minimally acceptable level, and it could result in *major* consequences on overall effectiveness.

Required-upon-Entry Ratings: Competencies

Participants rated if proficiency in each competency was required upon entry into an HR job at the identified career level. Participants provided this rating for all nine competencies.

Table 1.4. Required-upon-Entry Rating Scale

Required-upon-Entry Rating Anchors	
Is this competency required when entering an HR job at the <identified career level> level?	
Rating	**Response Scale Anchor**
0	**Not Required upon Entry/Time of Hire** An individual is not expected to enter the HR profession at the <identified career level> level with this competency. Experience on the job, or training, is the primary method for becoming proficient in this area. **An individual would be considered qualified to enter the HR profession even if the individual did NOT have this competency at the time of hire.**
1	**Required upon Entry/Time of Hire** An individual is expected to enter the HR profession at the <identified career level> level with this competency. Significant job training and time on the job are *not* provided to the individual to help him/her acquire and become proficient in this area, or job training or experience would not significantly increase one's proficiency in this area. **An individual would be considered qualified to enter the HR profession only if the individual had this competency at the time of hire.**

Results of the Content Validation Survey

This section presents the results of the Content Validation Survey sent to SHRM members. For each competency the overall results are presented, followed by results for the key behaviors, and then results for subgroups (i.e., career level, FTEs and work sector). As shown in Table 1.3 in previous section, importance ratings were made on a 4-point Likert scale ranging from 0 to 3. Mean importance ratings greater than or equal to 1.5, but less than 2.49, are considered "important," and mean importance ratings scored greater than or equal to 2.50 are considered "critical." Importance ratings are accompanied by standard deviation (SD)[1] values in parentheses. For example, "(M = 2.2, SD = .67)" indicates that the item was rated as important (2.2 on a 0-3 scale) and that the SD of these ratings is .67. A percentage (%) is reported to indicate the proportion of respondents who indicated that the competency is required upon entry into an HR job (see Table 1.4). A summary of these findings can be found in the Appendix of this document.

Human Resource Expertise (HR Knowledge)

HR professionals directly affect organizational success by developing, maintaining and executing sound human resource management (HRM) policies, practices and procedures (Pfeffer, 1998) that support organizational mission and goals. Effective HRM practices can have numerous benefits for organizations, for example, reduced turnover, increased productivity and financial performance, and sustained competitive advantage (e.g., Becker & Gerhart, 1996; Huselid, 1995). To implement successful initiatives, HR professionals must have a well-developed knowledge base about HRM practices. This knowledge is reflected in the *Human Resource Expertise* competency.

Through its specificity to the HR profession, *Human Resource Expertise* describes the knowledge needed by HR professionals to design, enact, evaluate and maintain sound HRM practices. This knowledge base includes the policies, practices, laws/regulations and principles that underlie effective HRM practices. As a technical competency, *Human Resource Expertise* serves as the driver of other behavioral competencies, such as *Business Acumen*, *Critical Evaluation* and *Consultation*. For example, an HR professional might convey his or her knowledge about effective HRM practices through a behavioral competency such as *Communication* or *Consultation*.

> *Human Resource Expertise* is defined as the knowledge of principles, practices and functions of effective human resource management.

---

[1] Standard deviation (SD) is the average extent to which ratings deviate from the mean. An SD value closer to zero indicates less deviation from the mean, whereas a larger SD value indicates more deviation from the mean. In other words, a smaller SD indicates that participants' ratings were more similar to one another whereas a larger SD indicates that participants' ratings were less similar to one another's.

Competency Ratings

Overall results for the *Human Resource Expertise* competency are presented in Table 2.1. These results indicate that this competency was rated as critical to the performance of HR professionals (M = 2.5, SD = .58). Further, 90% of respondents stated that proficiency in this competency is required upon entry into an HR job.

Table 2.1. Human Resource Expertise: Competency Summary

Rating	Mean (SD)
Importance	2.5 (.58)
Required upon entry	90%

Key Behaviors

Table 2.2 provides the mean importance ratings of behaviors associated with *Human Resource Expertise*. These behaviors reflect the need of an HR professional to maintain appropriate knowledge of a variety of relevant topics (e.g., "Remains current on relevant laws, legal rulings and regulations") and to apply this knowledge to create sound organizational practices and policies (e.g., "Develops and utilizes best practices"). All behaviors were rated as important or critical to HR success, with the lowest rating being 2.2 and the highest a 2.6. These high ratings indicate that these behaviors, associated with *Human Resource Expertise*, are necessary for success as an HR professional.

Table 2.2. Key Behaviors of Human Resource Expertise

Key Behaviors	Mean (SD)
Remains current on relevant laws, legal rulings and regulations.	2.6 (.57)
Maintains up-to-date knowledge of general HR practices, strategy and technology.	2.5 (.56)
Demonstrates a working knowledge of critical human resource functions, including strategy; workforce management; learning and development; total rewards; risk management; employment law; HR technology; and global and international HR.	2.5 (.59)
Prioritizes work duties for maximum efficiency.	2.4 (.59)
Develops and utilizes best practices.	2.3 (.56)
Delivers customized human resource solutions for organizational challenges.	2.3 (.64)
Seeks professional HR development.	2.2 (.61)
Seeks process improvement through numerous resources.	2.2 (.59)
Utilizes core business and HR-specific technologies to solve business challenges.	2.2 (.62)

Competency Ratings by Subgroups

Because the importance and necessity of the *Human Resource Expertise* competency may differ across demographic and organizational characteristics, more specific analyses of importance and required-upon-entry ratings are presented below.

Career Level

Table 2.3 presents the importance and required-upon-entry ratings for *Human Resource Expertise* at each of the four HR career levels. HR professionals at all career levels rated this competency as important or critical to job success, although this competency is viewed as most important at more senior career levels (i.e., senior and executive levels) than at junior career levels (i.e., early-career level and mid level). Additionally, more HR professionals indicated that this competency is important upon entering an executive-level job (94%) than an early-career job (44%).

A large increase in both importance and required-upon-entry ratings is seen between the early-career and mid-level ratings. Presumably, this occurs as the result of an increase in responsibility, the expansion of managerial responsibilities and a move from transactional to more strategic job responsibilities. It is also possible that early-career-level professionals are expected to develop this competency through on-the-job training or more formalized training and educational opportunities (e.g., conferences, workshops). These career level differences suggest that the *Human Resource Expertise* competency is important across all career levels and becomes more important, and a requisite qualification, at more senior career levels.

Table 2.3. Results by Career Level

Career Level	Importance	Required upon Entry
	Mean *(SD)*	% Yes
Early	1.8 *(.74)*	44
Mid	2.2 *(.55)*	86
Senior	2.7 *(.50)*	95
Executive	2.8 *(.43)*	94

Note: Importance was measured with a 4-point scale ranging from 0 (unimportant) to 3 (critical).

Full-Time Equivalents

Table 2.4 presents the importance and required-upon-entry ratings for *Human Resource Expertise* for organizations of varying staff sizes. These results show that this competency was rated as critical to HR performance and is required upon entry in most organizations. Additionally, the minimal variance in ratings across different numbers of FTEs indicates that *Human Resource Expertise* is critical to HR professionals' job success and is needed upon entry in the vast majority of organizations regardless of size.

Table 2.4. Results by Full-Time Equivalents

Full-Time Equivalents	Importance	Required upon Entry
	Mean *(SD)*	% Yes
1-99	2.5 *(.60)*	88
100-499	2.5 *(.57)*	91
500-2,499	2.6 *(.56)*	92
2,500-24,999	2.6 *(.54)*	92
≥25,000	2.6 *(.56)*	89

Note: Importance was measured with a 4-point scale ranging from 0 (unimportant) to 3 (critical).

Sector

Table 2.5 presents the importance and required-upon-entry ratings for *Human Resource Expertise* for organizations in different sectors. Across all work sectors this competency was rated as critical and required upon entry in most organizations. Additionally, these ratings show almost no variance across work sectors, which indicates that *Human Resource Expertise* is critical to HR professionals' job success and is required upon entry in nearly all organizations regardless of sector.

Table 2.5. Results by Work Sector

Work Sector	Importance	Required upon Entry
	Mean *(SD)*	% Yes
For-profit private	2.5 *(.58)*	90
For-profit public	2.5 *(.56)*	91
Government	2.5 *(.57)*	90
Nonprofit	2.5 *(.57)*	90
Other	2.5 *(.58)*	88

Note: Importance was measured with a 4-point scale ranging from 0 (unimportant) to 3 (critical).

Relationship Management

HR professionals regularly interact with clients and stakeholders; therefore, job success for an HR professional is largely a function of his or her ability to maintain productive interpersonal relationships and of his or her ability to help others do the same, or to display competency at *Relationship Management*.

Research has documented positive outcomes associated with productive and healthy interpersonal relationships in the work environment (Reich & Hershcovis, 2011). Positive, formal relationships (e.g., an employee's relationship with his or her supervisor) are associated with beneficial outcomes for employees, such as improved feelings of belonging and inclusion in the workplace (Alvesson & Sveningsson, 2003), increased salary, increased promotions, greater career mobility and other rewards (Allen, Eby, Poteet, Lima, & Lentz, 2004). Positive, informal relationships at work are associated with greater job satisfaction, involvement, performance, team cohesion, organizational commitment, positive work atmosphere and lessened turnover intentions (Berman, West, & Richter, 2002). Employees who have better interpersonal relationships with their co-workers and supervisors may also perceive the organization as more supportive (Wallace, Edwards, Arnold, Frazier, & Finch, 2009), may be more committed to their organization and may experience increased perceptions of fit within their organizations (Kristof-Brown, Zimmerman, & Johnson, 2005). In sum, healthy interpersonal relationships among employees at an organization contribute positively to an employee's and organization's success.

> *Relationship Management is defined as the ability to manage interactions to provide service and to support the organization.*

Competency Ratings

Overall results for the *Relationship Management* competency are presented in Table 3.1. Results indicate that this competency was rated as critical to the performance of HR professionals (M = 2.5, SD = .55), and 91% of respondents rated proficiency in this competency as required upon entry into an HR job. These findings reflect the large extent to which HR professionals must interact with others and the HR professionals' position in influencing interpersonal relationships throughout an organization.

Table 3.1. Relationship Management: Competency Summary

Ratings	Mean *(SD)*
Importance	2.5 *(.55)*
Required upon entry	91%

Key Behaviors

Table 3.2 provides the mean importance ratings of behaviors associated with *Relationship Management*. These behaviors reflect the need of HR professionals to manage their own relationships (e.g., "Treats all stakeholders with respect and dignity") and facilitate others' relationships (e.g., "Fosters effective teambuilding among stakeholders"). All behaviors were rated between 2.2 and 2.8, indicating that these behaviors are important or critical for success as an HR professional.

Table 3.2. Key Behaviors of Relationship Management

Key Behaviors	Mean (SD)
Establishes credibility in all interactions.	2.8 (.44)
Treats all stakeholders with respect and dignity.	2.7 (.45)
Builds engaging relationships with all organizational stakeholders through trust, teamwork and direct communication.	2.6 (.52)
Demonstrates approachability and openness.	2.6 (.53)
Ensures alignment within HR when delivering services and information to the organization.	2.5 (.55)
Provides customer service to organizational stakeholders.	2.5 (.58)
Promotes successful relationships with stakeholders.	2.5 (.57)
Manages internal and external relationships in ways that promote the best interests of all parties.	2.4 (.56)
Champions the view that organizational effectiveness benefits all stakeholders.	2.3 (.62)
Serves as an advocate when appropriate.	2.3 (.59)
Fosters effective teambuilding among stakeholders.	2.3 (.61)
Demonstrates ability to effectively build a network of contacts at all levels within the HR function and in the community, both internally and externally.	2.2 (.63)

Competency Ratings by Subgroups

Because the importance and necessity of the *Relationship Management* competency may differ across demographic and organizational characteristics, more specific analyses of importance and required-upon-entry ratings are presented below.

Career Level

Table 3.3 presents the importance and required-upon-entry ratings for each of the four HR career levels. HR professionals at all career levels rated *Relationship Management* as important or critical to job success for HR professionals. However, the importance ratings of this competency steadily increase with career level, and this competency is rated as more important at senior levels (i.e., senior and executive) than at junior levels (i.e., early and mid). Additionally, more HR professionals indicated that this competency is required upon entering an executive-level job (96%) than an early-career job (73%). The largest increase in required-upon-entry ratings is seen between the early-career and mid-level ratings. This finding may indicate that early-career HR professionals are expected to develop and refine this competency as they begin their careers.

Table 3.3. Results by Career Level

Career Level	Importance Mean (SD)	Required upon Entry % Yes
Early	2.1 (.65)	73
Mid	2.3 (.57)	86
Senior	2.6 (.52)	94
Executive	2.7 (.47)	96

Note: Importance was measured with a 4-point scale ranging from 0 (unimportant) to 3 (critical).

Full-Time Equivalents

Table 3.4 presents the importance and required-upon-entry ratings for *Relationship Management* for organizations of varying staff sizes. Across all organization sizes this competency was rated as both critical and required upon entry. These results also show almost no variance across number of FTEs for importance ratings and only minor differences for required-upon-entry ratings. This outcome suggests that, regardless of the number of FTEs, *Relationship Management* is not only critical to HR professionals' job success but is also required upon entry in nearly all organizations.

Table 3.4. Results by Full-Time Equivalents

Full-Time Equivalents	Importance	Required upon Entry
	Mean *(SD)*	% Yes
1-99	2.5 *(.57)*	90
100-499	2.5 *(.55)*	92
500-2,499	2.5 *(.55)*	92
2,500-24,999	2.6 *(.53)*	92
≥25,000	2.5 *(.54)*	91

Note: Importance was measured with a 4-point scale ranging from 0 (unimportant) to 3 (critical).

Sector

Table 3.5 presents the importance and required-upon-entry ratings for *Relationship Management* for organizations in different sectors. These ratings show no differences across work sectors for importance ratings, with all mean ratings indicating that *Relationship Management* is critical, and only minor differences for required-upon-entry ratings. Together these findings indicate that, regardless of sector, *Relationship Management* is important to HR professionals' job success and is required upon entry in nearly all organizations.

Table 3.5. Results by Work Sector

Work Sector	Importance	Required upon Entry
	Mean *(SD)*	% Yes
For-profit private	2.5 *(.56)*	91
For-profit public	2.5 *(.55)*	92
Government	2.5 *(.56)*	91
Nonprofit	2.5 *(.55)*	92
Other	2.5 *(.54)*	92

Note: Importance was measured with a 4-point scale ranging from 0 (unimportant) to 3 (critical).

Consultation

Within their own organizations, HR professionals often take on the role of an internal consultant or expert on human capital issues. In this role, HR professionals can help business units address challenges related to human capital, such as staffing needs, training and development needs, employee performance issues, and employee relations issues (Combs, Liu, Hall, & Ketchen, 2006). To be a successful human capital expert, HR professionals must not only possess requisite knowledge about HRM practices but also be able to provide guidance to internal stakeholders. The most effective HR professionals possess a specific set of attributes that enables them to translate complicated information about HRM practices (i.e., *Human Resource Expertise*) into actionable recommendations for end users (e.g., hiring managers). HR professionals must be able to analyze business challenges, generate creative solutions, and provide accurate and timely guidance to internal stakeholders based on best practices and research that account for the distinct internal and external environment of the organization.

Consultation is defined as the ability to provide guidance to organizational stakeholders.

Competency Ratings

Overall results for the *Consultation* competency are presented in Table 4.1. This competency was rated as important to the performance of HR professionals (M = 2.3, SD = .66), and 80% of respondents indicated that proficiency in *Consultation* is required upon entry into an HR job. However, these overall results mask the fact that ratings for this competency are strongly influenced by career level (discussed below). Career level differences likely explain the lower ratings, compared to other competencies, in the other breakouts for this competency (i.e., FTEs and work sector). Regardless, these overall ratings still confirm the importance of this competency and its necessity upon entry into HR positions in light of HR's role as organizational experts in human capital issues.

Table 4.1. Consultation: Competency Summary

Ratings	Mean *(SD)*
Importance	2.3 *(.66)*
Required upon entry	80%

Key Behaviors

Table 4.2 displays the mean importance ratings of behaviors associated with *Consultation*—these ratings ranged from 1.8 to 2.4. These behaviors represent HR professionals' ability to apply HR and human capital knowledge to address organizational needs (e.g., "Analyzes specific business challenges involving workforce and offers solutions based upon best practices or research"). All of these behaviors were rated as important to successful HR job performance.

Table 4.2. Key Behaviors of Consultation

Key Behaviors	Mean *(SD)*
Applies creative problem-solving to address business needs and issues.	2.4 *(.60)*
Serves as an in-house workforce and people management expert.	2.3 *(.66)*
Analyzes specific business challenges involving the workforce and offers solutions based on best practices or research.	2.3 *(.65)*
Generates specific organizational interventions (e.g., culture change, change management, restructuring, training) to support organizational objectives.	2.3 *(.69)*
Develops consultative and coaching skills.	2.3 *(.64)*
Guides employees regarding specific career situations.	1.8 *(.66)*

Competency Ratings by Subgroups

Because the importance and necessity of the *Consultation* competency may differ across demographic and organizational characteristics, more specific analyses of importance and required-upon-entry ratings are presented below.

Career Level

Table 4.3 shows the importance and required-upon-entry ratings for each of the four HR career levels. HR professionals at all career levels indicated that *Consultation* is important or critical to job success. However, the importance ratings of this competency increase substantially from early-career level to the executive level (a rating of 1.5 for early-career level and a rating of 2.6 for executive level). A similar pattern of results is also found for required-upon-entry ratings; specifically, more HR professionals indicated that this competency is required upon entering an executive-level job (91%) than an early-career-level job (34%).

An increase in both importance and required-upon-entry ratings is seen between early and mid levels and between mid and senior levels. These large increases might be explained by the nature of HR jobs at these levels. Early-career HR professionals will likely have fewer consultative responsibilities; they may instead be expected to begin developing these skills as they support more experienced HR professionals. Further, given the moderate required-upon-entry and importance ratings for mid-level HR professionals, it is likely that *Consultation* becomes a larger part of the job for mid-level professionals. In sum, *Consultation* may not necessarily be expected upon entry into early or mid-level jobs, but it is expected for senior- and executive-level jobs. Despite these career level differences, these results support the importance of *Consultation* to HR job success and position it as a critical area for development in early and mid-level HR professionals who wish to advance their careers.

Table 4.3. Results by Career Level

Career Level	Importance	Required upon Entry
	Mean *(SD)*	% Yes
Early	1.5 *(.85)*	34
Mid	2.1 *(.66)*	67
Senior	2.4 *(.56)*	89
Executive	2.6 *(.53)*	91

Note: Importance was measured with a 4-point scale ranging from 0 (unimportant) to 3 (critical).

Full-Time Equivalents

Table 4.4 presents the importance and required-upon-entry ratings for *Consultation* in organizations of varying staff sizes. Importance ratings show little variance according to the number of FTEs, with all ratings indicating that *Consultation* is important to job performance for HR professionals and required upon entry in most organizations. Minor differences are seen with regard to the required-upon-entry ratings, especially when comparing small organizations (1-99 FTEs) with larger organizations. However, these differences are relatively minor (maximum difference of 6%) and do not change the overall conclusion that *Consultation* is important to HR professionals' job success and is required upon entry in most organizations regardless of the number of FTEs.

Table 4.4. Results by Full-Time Equivalents

Full-Time Equivalents	Importance	Required upon Entry
	Mean *(SD)*	% Yes
1-99	2.3 *(.67)*	78
100-499	2.4 *(.60)*	82
500-2,499	2.3 *(.65)*	81
2,500-24,999	2.4 *(.62)*	84
>25,000	2.4 *(.64)*	82

Note: Importance was measured with a 4-point scale ranging from 0 (unimportant) to 3 (critical).

Sector

Table 4.5 presents the importance and required-upon-entry ratings for *Consultation* for organizations in different sectors. These ratings indicate that this competency is important and required upon entry in most organizations across all work sectors. Additionally, there were almost no differences in ratings across work sectors, indicating that sector has little impact on the importance and necessity of *Consultation* for HR professionals.

Table 4.5. Results by Work Sector

Work Sector	Importance	Required upon Entry
	Mean (SD)	% Yes
For-profit private	2.3 *(.66)*	80
For-profit public	2.4 *(.64)*	82
Government	2.4 *(.64)*	81
Nonprofit	2.3 *(.65)*	81
Other	2.3 *(.66)*	79

Note: Importance was measured with a 4-point scale ranging from 0 (unimportant) to 3 (critical).

Leadership and Navigation

Effective leaders are associated with numerous positive outcomes (Barling, Christie, & Hoption, 2010), for example, positive employee work attitudes such as job satisfaction and organizational commitment (Burke, Sims, Lazzara, & Salas, 2007; Judge & Piccolo, 2004), decreased turnover and increased employee job performance (Barling et al., 2011). HR professionals at each career level can demonstrate *Leadership and Navigation*. For example, early-career HR professionals can demonstrate proficiency in this competency by behaving in ways consistent with organizational culture and by fostering collaboration with co-workers. Mid- and senior-level HR professionals may develop strategies to implement HR initiatives, and serve as a supporter of the initiatives of others. Executive-level leaders not only establish a vision for HR initiatives but also work to obtain the buy-in of relevant stakeholders, serve as transformational leaders to implement change and lead the organization in the face of adversity. In summary, *Leadership and Navigation* recognizes this vital role for HR professionals by describing the attributes needed by HR professionals to lead organizational initiatives and obtain buy-in from stakeholders.

> Leadership and Navigation is defined as the ability to direct and contribute to initiatives and processes within the organization.

Competency Ratings

Overall results for *Leadership and Navigation* are presented in Table 5.1. These results indicate that this competency was rated as important to the performance of HR professionals (M = 2.2, SD = .73). Further, 67% of respondents indicated that proficiency in this competency is required upon entry into an HR job. Similar to the results for *Consultation*, the overall rating is somewhat misleading because ratings are largely influenced by career level (discussed further below). As well as influencing the overall ratings, these career level differences likely explain the lower ratings for other breakouts (i.e., FTEs and work sector) compared with other competencies. Regardless, these results still reflect the strong organizational visibility of HR programs and activities, the impact HR can have on other organizational stakeholders, and the overall importance of *Leadership and Navigation* to the performance of HR professionals.

Table 5.1. Leadership and Navigation: Competency Summary

Ratings	Mean *(SD)*
Importance	2.2 *(.73)*
Required upon entry	67%

Key Behaviors

Table 5.2 provides the mean importance ratings of behaviors associated with *Leadership and Navigation*. These behaviors represent the need for HR professionals to develop and implement strategy that aligns with the organization's mission (e.g., "Exhibits behaviors consistent with and conforming to organizational culture"), for HR professionals to establish and foster a productive organizational environment (e.g., "Fosters collaboration"), and for HR professionals to demonstrate the ability to accomplish goals even during challenging times (e.g., "Develops solutions to overcome potential obstacles to successful implementation of initiatives"). All the ratings for these behaviors fell between 2.2 and 2.5, indicating that they are all important or critical to the success of HR professionals.

Table 5.2. Key Behaviors of Leadership and Navigation

Key Behaviors	Mean *(SD)*
Exhibits behaviors consistent with and conforming to organizational culture.	2.5 *(.58)*
Fosters collaboration.	2.4 *(.58)*
Understands the most effective and efficient way to accomplish tasks within the parameters of organizational hierarchy, processes, systems and policies.	2.4 *(.58)*
Develops solutions to overcome potential obstacles to successful implementation of initiatives.	2.4 *(.59)*
Demonstrates agility and expertise when leading organizational initiatives or when supporting the initiatives of others.	2.3 *(.59)*
Sets the vision for HR initiatives and builds buy-in from internal and external stakeholders.	2.3 *(.76)*
Leads the organization through adversity with resilience and tenacity.	2.3 *(.71)*
Promotes consensus among organizational stakeholders (e.g., employees, business unit leaders, informal leaders) when proposing new initiatives.	2.3 *(.63)*
Serves as a transformational leader for the organization by leading change.	2.2 *(.73)*

Competency Ratings by Subgroups

Because the importance and necessity of the *Leadership and Navigation* competency may differ across demographic and organizational characteristics, more specific analyses of importance and required-upon-entry ratings are presented below.

Career Level

Table 5.3 presents the importance and required-upon-entry ratings for each of the four HR career levels. Early-career respondents indicated that this competency is not important (mean rating of 1.3) to HR performance. However, other career levels rated *Leadership and Navigation* as important (mid and senior levels) or critical (executive level) to performance as an HR professional at these respective career levels. Similarly, early and mid-level professionals rated *Leadership and Navigation* as a competency that is not necessarily required upon entry, whereas senior- and executive-level professionals were much more likely to indicate that this competency is required upon entry into an HR job at those career levels.

These large differences in ratings might be explained by the changing nature of HR jobs across career levels. It is less likely that early-career-level professionals will have leadership responsibilities; instead, HR professionals at more junior career levels are often engaged in transactional work. At the mid level, HR professionals might begin to take on leadership responsibilities, but even at this level, HR professionals are likely to be continuing to develop their leadership competence on the job or through formal training programs. It is not until the senior level that HR professionals are expected to have fine-tuned their leadership capabilities, and at the executive level, leadership is important to the job and required for entry. Overall, these results indicate that the *Leadership and Navigation* competency contributes to HR job performance, albeit differently across career levels, and provides a clear area of development for early and mid-level HR professionals who wish to advance their careers and move into more senior positions.

Table 5.3. Results by Career Level

Career Level	Importance Mean *(SD)*	Required upon Entry % Yes
Early	1.3 *(.87)*	24
Mid	1.7 *(.70)*	41
Senior	2.3 *(.58)*	78
Executive	2.6 *(.51)*	90

Note: Importance was measured with a 4-point scale ranging from 0 (unimportant) to 3 (critical).

Full-Time Equivalents

Table 5.4 presents the importance and required-upon-entry ratings for *Leadership and Navigation* for organizations of varying staff sizes. Ratings across all organization sizes indicate that this competency is important for HR professionals and is required in a majority of organizations. Additionally, these results show little variance according to the number of FTEs for both importance and required-upon-entry ratings, although HR professionals in smaller organizations (1-99 FTEs) were less likely to indicate that this competency is required upon entry as their counterparts in larger organizations (e.g., 2,500-24,999 FTEs). Regardless, this difference is relatively minor (maximum difference of 8%), and these findings indicate that *Leadership and Navigation* is important to HR professionals' job success and is required upon entry in most organizations regardless of the number of FTEs.

Table 5.4. Results by Full-Time Equivalents

Full-Time Equivalents	Importance Mean *(SD)*	Required upon Entry % Yes
1-99	2.1 *(.75)*	65
100-499	2.2 *(.73)*	66
500-2,499	2.2 *(.73)*	68
2,500-24,999	2.3 *(.68)*	73
>25,000	2.3 *(.70)*	69

Note: Importance was measured with a 4-point scale ranging from 0 (unimportant) to 3 (critical).

Sector

Table 5.5 presents the importance and required-upon-entry ratings for *Leadership and Navigation* for organizations in different sectors. Across all sectors this competency was rated as important to HR performance, and the majority of respondents indicated that proficiency in this competency is required upon entry into an HR job. Additionally, these ratings show only minor differences across sectors.

Table 5.5. Results by Work Sector

Work Sector	Importance Mean *(SD)*	Required upon Entry % Yes
For-profit private	2.1 *(.74)*	66
For-profit public	2.2 *(.71)*	68
Government	2.2 *(.73)*	67
Nonprofit	2.2 *(.73)*	67
Other	2.2 *(.74)*	66

Note: Importance was measured with a 4-point scale ranging from 0 (unimportant) to 3 (critical).

Communication

Effective communication is one of the building blocks of personal and career success (Showry & Manasa, 2012). This is particularly true for HR professionals. At more junior career levels, HR professionals may need to field employee grievances, conduct investigations and intervene to resolve employee interpersonal challenges. More senior-level HR professionals are often required to interact with a variety of stakeholders to develop, interpret and distribute policy and initiative information to employees and to collaborate with other organizational units to address business challenges from a human capital perspective. Especially at senior and executive career levels, effective communication is essential for sharing the leader's vision and the organization's mission, describing new initiatives, setting goals and communicating progress. When HR information is communicated well, employees better understand the purpose and value of policies and practices. For example, when managers adeptly communicate HR practices and policies to their employees, employees perceive the organization's HRM to be more effective, and in turn employee satisfaction and business unit performance are positively affected (Den Hartog, Boon, Verburg, & Croon, 2013).

> Communication is defined as the ability to effectively exchange information with stakeholders.

To competently fulfill duties at each career level, HR professionals must ensure that the messages they distribute are clear, concise and readily understood. In summary, proficiency in *Communication* is mandatory for the success of HR professionals.

Competency Ratings

Results for the *Communication* competency are presented in Table 6.1. This competency was rated as critical to the performance of HR professionals (M = 2.5, SD = .58), and 90% of respondents indicated that proficiency in this competency is required upon entry into an HR job. These findings reflect HR professionals' integral role as receivers and distributors of a large amount of information, requiring high levels of interpersonal interaction.

Table 6.1. Communication: Competency Summary

Rating	Mean *(SD)*
Importance	2.5 *(.58)*
Required upon entry	90%

Key Behaviors

Table 6.2 provides the mean importance ratings of behaviors associated with *Communication*. These behaviors reflect the need for HR professionals to disseminate information to stakeholders (e.g., "Provides clear, concise information to others in verbal, written, electronic and other communication formats for public and organizational consumption"). These behaviors also reflect the need for HR professionals to engage in productive conversations with stakeholders seeking HR's services (e.g., "Provides constructive feedback effectively" and "Demonstrates an understanding of the audience's perspective") and to help ensure quality communication among organizational stakeholders (e.g., "Helps others consider new perspectives"). The relatively high ratings for these behaviors, with mean ratings ranging from 2.1 to 2.6, indicate that these behaviors are important or critical to effective job performance for HR professionals.

Table 6.2. Key Behaviors of Communication

Key Behaviors	Mean *(SD)*
Provides clear, concise information to others in verbal, written, electronic and other communication formats for public and organizational consumption.	2.6 *(.53)*
Listens actively and empathetically to the views of others.	2.6 *(.52)*
Delivers critical information to all stakeholders.	2.5 *(.64)*
Seeks further information to clarify ambiguity.	2.5 *(.55)*
Provides constructive feedback effectively.	2.4 *(.56)*
Ensures effective communication throughout the organization.	2.4 *(.62)*
Provides thoughtful feedback in appropriate situations.	2.4 *(.56)*
Provides proactive communications.	2.4 *(.55)*
Demonstrates an understanding of the audience's perspective.	2.4 *(.55)*
Treats constructive feedback as a developmental opportunity.	2.4 *(.57)*
Welcomes the opportunity to discuss competing points of view.	2.3 *(.60)*
Helps others consider new perspectives.	2.2 *(.59)*
Leads effective and efficient meetings.	2.2 *(.62)*
Helps managers communicate not just on HR issues.	2.1 *(.64)*

Competency Ratings by Subgroups

Because the importance and necessity of the *Communication* competency may differ across demographic and organizational characteristics, more specific analyses of importance and required-upon-entry ratings are presented below.

Career Level

The importance and required-upon-entry ratings for each of the four HR career levels are presented in Table 6.3. HR professionals at all career levels indicated that *Communication* is important or critical to job success. The importance ratings increase slightly with career level, such that ratings are higher for more senior career levels than for junior career levels. Additionally, more HR professionals indicated that this competency is important when entering an executive-level job (95%) than an early-career job (77%). Although *Communication* is required upon entry at all career levels, the moderate difference in required-upon-entry ratings across career levels suggests that HR professionals are expected to develop this competency throughout their careers.

Table 6.3. Results by Career Level

Career Level	Importance	Required upon Entry
	Mean *(SD)*	% Yes
Early	2.1 *(.72)*	77
Mid	2.3 *(.61)*	85
Senior	2.5 *(.54)*	93
Executive	2.6 *(.50)*	95

Note: Importance was measured with a 4-point scale ranging from 0 (unimportant) to 3 (critical).

Full-Time Equivalents

Table 6.4 presents the importance and required-upon-entry ratings for *Communication* in organizations of varying staff sizes. These results show essentially no difference according to number of FTEs, and ratings indicate that this competency is both critical to job success and required upon entry in nearly all organizations.

Table 6.4. Results by Full-Time Equivalents

Full-Time Equivalents	Importance	Required upon Entry
	Mean *(SD)*	% Yes
1-99	2.5 *(.59)*	90
100-499	2.5 *(.57)*	90
500-2,499	2.5 *(.58)*	91
2,500-24,999	2.5 *(.56)*	91
>25,000	2.5 *(.57)*	91

Note: Importance was measured with a 4-point scale ranging from 0 (unimportant) to 3 (critical).

Sector

Table 6.5 presents the importance and required-upon-entry ratings for *Communication* for organizations in different sectors. Similar to the results for FTEs, there are basically no differences in ratings across sectors. This competency was rated as critical to the success of HR professionals and was rated as required upon entry in nearly all organizations regardless of sector.

Table 6.5. Results by Work Sector

Work Sector	Importance	Required upon Entry
	Mean *(SD)*	% Yes
For-profit private	2.5 *(.59)*	90
For-profit public	2.5 *(.57)*	91
Government	2.5 *(.56)*	91
Nonprofit	2.5 *(.57)*	91
Other	2.5 *(.57)*	91

Note: Importance was measured with a 4-point scale ranging from 0 (unimportant) to 3 (critical).

Global and Cultural Effectiveness

Diversity within a team or organization can facilitate success by fostering creativity, promoting healthy working relationships and equipping organizations with an opportunity to connect with a wider audience (Jayne & Dipboye, 2004). Because many organizations are proactively attempting to increase the diversity of their workforces, and because of today's increasingly global workforce, HR professionals must be able to effectively and respectfully interact with colleagues, customers and clients of varying backgrounds and cultures.

HR professionals are at the forefront of these changes. For example, an increasing number of organizations choose to invest in diversity initiatives, such as diversity training, to facilitate successful interpersonal interactions among members of varying cultures (Kulik & Roberson, 2008). In fact, 67% of U.S. organizations and 74% of *Fortune* 500 companies use diversity training programs (Kimley, 1997). HR professionals are often tasked with developing, delivering and evaluating these diversity-related initiatives. Additionally, various laws and regulations also require organizations to employ inclusive hiring practices. Again, HR professionals are often primarily responsible for complying with these laws and regulations given their pivotal role in employee hiring. Because of the role of HR professionals in promoting and maintaining a diverse workforce, it is easy to see the importance of *Global and Cultural Effectiveness* for HR professionals.

> *Global and Cultural Effectiveness* is defined as the ability to value and consider the perspectives and backgrounds of all parties.

Competency Ratings

Overall results for *Global and Cultural Effectiveness* are presented in Table 7.1. These results indicate that this competency was rated as important to the performance of HR professionals (M = 1.9, SD = .72), although the relatively large standard deviation suggests a significant amount of disagreement among respondents with regard to these ratings. Additionally, only 57% of respondents indicated that proficiency in this competency is required upon entry into an HR job. It seems likely that disagreement about the importance of this competency for HR performance is also reflected in disagreement about the importance of this competency upon entry. Overall, these results indicate that *Global and Cultural Effectiveness* is a bit less important than other competencies for HR job success, although there is a fair amount of disagreement among respondents about this, and it may not be a principal competency for entry into an HR position.

Table 7.1. Global and Cultural Effectiveness: Competency Summary

Rating	Mean *(SD)*
Importance	1.9 *(.72)*
Required upon entry	57%

Key Behaviors

Table 7.2 provides the mean importance ratings of behaviors for *Global and Cultural Effectiveness*. These behaviors reflect HR professionals' need to maintain an open mind when interacting with individuals who have perspectives different from their own (e.g., "Maintains openness to others' ideas and makes decisions based on experience, data, facts and reasoned judgment"). These behaviors also reflect the need for HR professionals to respect cross-cultural differences and value the cultural identity of employees (e.g., "Appreciates the commonalities, values and individual uniqueness of all human beings"). With regard to the importance ratings of these behaviors, the mean ratings ranged from 1.9 to 2.6, which indicate that these behaviors are important or critical for successful HR professionals.

Table 7.2. Key Behaviors of Global and Cultural Effectiveness

Key Behaviors	Mean *(SD)*
Has a strong set of core values while operating with adaptability to particular conditions, situations and people.	2.6 *(.56)*
Maintains openness to others' ideas and makes decisions based on experience, data, facts and reasoned judgment.	2.5 *(.54)*
Demonstrates nonjudgmental respect for other perspectives.	2.5 *(.58)*
Works effectively with diverse cultures and populations.	2.4 *(.58)*
Conducts business with an understanding and respect for the differences in rules, customs, laws, regulations and business operations between own culture and all cultures.	2.4 *(.62)*
Appreciates the commonalities, values and individual uniqueness of all human beings.	2.4 *(.61)*
Possesses self-awareness and humility to learn from others.	2.4 *(.60)*
Embraces inclusion.	2.3 *(.62)*
Adapts perspective and behavior to meet the cultural context.	2.2 *(.60)*
Navigates the differences between commonly accepted practice and law when conducting business in other nations.	2.2 *(.76)*
Operates with a global, open mindset while being sensitive to local cultural issues and needs.	2.2 *(.65)*
Operates with a fundamental trust in other human beings.	2.2 *(.66)*
Takes the responsibility to teach others about the differences and benefits that multiple cultures bring to the organization to ensure inclusion.	2.0 *(.68)*
Incorporates global business and economic trends into business decisions.	1.9 *(.74)*

Competency Ratings by Subgroups

Because the importance and necessity of the *Global and Cultural Effectiveness* competency may differ across demographic and organizational characteristics, more specific analyses of importance and required-upon-entry ratings are presented below.

Career Level

Table 7.3 presents the importance and required-upon-entry ratings for each of the four HR career levels. HR professionals at all career levels indicated that *Global and Cultural Effectiveness* is important to job success. However, the importance ratings increase to some degree with career level, such that this competency is rated as more important for more senior career levels than for more junior career levels. Additionally, more HR professionals indicated that this competency is needed upon entering an executive-level job (66%) than an early-career-level job (41%). Together, these results suggest that although *Global and Cultural Effectiveness* is important to HR professionals regardless of career level, this competency is more important at advanced HR career levels (e.g., senior and executive levels) than at junior career levels.

Table 7.3. Results by Career Level

Career Level	Importance	Required upon Entry
	Mean *(SD)*	% Yes
Early	1.5 *(.87)*	41
Mid	1.7 *(.75)*	47
Senior	2.0 *(.65)*	60
Executive	2.1 *(.63)*	66

Note: Importance was measured with a 4-point scale ranging from 0 (unimportant) to 3 (critical).

Full-Time Equivalents

Table 7.4 presents the importance and required-upon-entry ratings for *Global and Cultural Effectiveness* for organizations of varying staff sizes. Across all categories of FTEs there are only minimal differences in importance ratings. All groups rated this competency as important, and a majority of respondents indicated that this competency is required upon entry.

Table 7.4. Results by Full-Time Equivalents

Full-Time Equivalents	Importance	Required upon Entry
	Mean *(SD)*	% Yes
1-99	1.9 *(.74)*	55
100-499	1.9 *(.71)*	57
500-2,499	1.9 *(.69)*	57
2,500-24,999	2.0 *(.67)*	60
≥25,000	2.0 *(.69)*	56

Note: Importance was measured with a 4-point scale ranging from 0 (unimportant) to 3 (critical).

Sector

Table 7.5 presents the importance and required-upon-entry ratings for *Global and Cultural Effectiveness* for organizations in different sectors. Similar to the results for FTEs, these results show little to no differences across sectors. Across all sectors this competency was rated as important to HR professionals' job performance, and a majority of respondents rated this competency as required upon entry.

Table 7.5. Results by Work Sector

Work Sector	Importance	Required upon Entry
	Mean *(SD)*	% Yes
For-profit private	1.9 *(.71)*	56
For-profit public	1.9 *(.68)*	57
Government	1.9 *(.73)*	58
Nonprofit	2.0 *(.73)*	60
Other	2.0 *(.70)*	60

Note: Importance was measured with a 4-point scale ranging from 0 (unimportant) to 3 (critical).

Ethical Practice

As with all other employees, it is crucial that HR professionals be ethical. HR professionals should consider the core values of their organizations and act with integrity. But beyond adhering to rigorous ethical standards themselves, HR professionals are often tasked with creating ethical HR systems or reinforcing an organization's ethical climate. These efforts serve several purposes, but most notably, implementing a strong ethical climate can help protect an organization from adverse employee behavior. And implementing ethical systems is essential to organizations because ethical HR systems are associated with higher levels of organizational performance (Lado & Wilson, 1994).

HR professionals at all career levels should not only adhere to their organization's ethical climate but help drive it as well. One such way that HR professionals can influence their organization's ethical climate is by responding to ethical issues (Bartels, Harrick, Martell, & Strickland, 1998). For example, early-career and mid-level HR professionals might be responsible for conducting thorough and confidential investigations into reports of unethical behavior and for recommending further action (e.g., suspension or termination of an employee). At more senior levels of experience, HR professionals might be responsible for ensuring that HR systems reinforce appropriate employee behaviors, values and norms that contribute to the organization's ethical climate. For example, senior-level HR professionals might develop effective policies and procedures for employees to report unethical behavior, or ensure that the requirements for determining promotions and pay raises are consistent throughout the organization and transparent for employees. In summary, successful HR professionals both adhere to ethical guidelines with regard to their own behavior and serve as drivers of an ethical climate in their organizations. To do this, HR employees must have thoroughly developed competence in *Ethical Practice*.

> *Ethical Practice* is defined as the ability to integrate core values, integrity and accountability throughout all organizational and business practices.

Competency Ratings

Results for *Ethical Practice* are presented in Table 8.1. These results indicate that this competency was rated as critical to the performance of HR professionals (M = 2.7, SD = .47), and 97% of respondents indicated that proficiency in this competency is required upon entry into an HR job. These findings reflect HR's central role in maintaining an organization's ethical climate.

Table 8.1. Ethical Practice: Competency Summary

Rating	Mean (SD)
Importance	2.7 (.47)
Required upon entry	97%

Key Behaviors

Table 8.2 provides the mean importance ratings of behaviors associated with *Ethical Practice*. These behaviors reflect the need for HR professionals to act ethically (e.g., "Maintains confidentiality"), to hold employees to the organizational code of ethics (e.g., "Responds immediately to all reports of unethical behavior or conflicts of interest"), and to establish and promote ethical practices across the organization (e.g., "Drives the corporate ethical environment"). Mean importance ratings on the behaviors associated with *Ethical Practice* ranged from 2.2 to 2.9, indicating that these behaviors are important or critical to the effective job performance of HR professionals.

Table 8.2. Key Behaviors of Ethical Practice

Key Behaviors	Mean (SD)
Maintains confidentiality.	2.9 (.27)
Acts with personal, professional and behavioral integrity.	2.9 (.35)
Responds immediately to all reports of unethical behavior or conflicts of interest.	2.8 (.47)
Empowers all employees to report unethical behavior or conflicts of interest without fear of reprisal.	2.7 (.51)
Shows consistency between espoused and enacted values.	2.6 (.54)
Acknowledges mistakes.	2.4 (.56)
Drives the corporate ethical environment.	2.4 (.66)
Applies power or authority appropriately.	2.4 (.60)
Recognizes personal bias and others' tendency toward bias, and takes measures to mitigate the influence of bias in business decisions.	2.4 (.57)
Maintains appropriate levels of transparency in organizational practices.	2.3 (.57)
Ensures that all stakeholder voices are heard.	2.2 (.60)
Manages political and social pressures when making decisions.	2.2 (.61)

Competency Ratings by Subgroups

Because the importance and necessity of the *Ethical Practice* competency may differ across demographic and organizational characteristics, more specific analyses of importance and required-upon-entry ratings are presented below.

Career Level

Table 8.3 presents the importance and required-upon-entry ratings for each of the four HR career levels. HR professionals at all career levels indicated that *Ethical Practice* is critical to job success, and these ratings increased slightly with career level. Additionally, only slightly more HR professionals indicated that this competency is required upon entering a job at the executive level (98%) than at the early-career level (90%). Together, these results suggest that *Ethical Practice* is critical to job success and required upon entry for HR professionals at all career levels.

Table 8.3. Results by Career Level

Career Level	Importance	Required upon Entry
	Mean (SD)	% Yes
Early	2.5 (.62)	90
Mid	2.6 (.52)	95
Senior	2.8 (.44)	97
Executive	2.9 (.35)	98

Note: Importance was measured with a 4-point scale ranging from 0 (unimportant) to 3 (critical).

Full-Time Equivalents

Table 8.4 presents the importance and required-upon-entry ratings for *Ethical Practice* for organizations of varying staff sizes. Across all organization sizes this competency was rated as critical for success and required upon entry into HR jobs. Additionally, these results show basically no difference according to number of FTEs, which indicates the importance of *Ethical Practice* regardless of organization size.

Table 8.4. Results by Full-Time Equivalents

Full-Time Equivalents	Importance	Required upon Entry
	Mean (SD)	% Yes
1-99	2.7 (.48)	96
100-499	2.8 (.47)	96
500-2,499	2.8 (.45)	97
2,500-24,999	2.8 (.44)	98
>25,000	2.8 (.44)	97

Note: Importance was measured with a 4-point scale ranging from 0 (unimportant) to 3 (critical).

Sector

Table 8.5 presents the importance and required-upon-entry ratings for *Ethical Practice* for organizations in different sectors. Similar to the results for number of FTEs, there are no differences in ratings across sectors, and HR professionals in all sectors rated this competency as critical to performance and required upon entry in nearly all organizations.

Table 8.5. Results by Work Sector

Work Sector	Importance	Required upon Entry
	Mean (SD)	% Yes
For-profit private	2.7 (.47)	97
For-profit public	2.8 (.45)	97
Government	2.8 (.46)	96
Nonprofit	2.8 (.45)	97
Other	2.8 (.44)	96

Note: Importance was measured with a 4-point scale ranging from 0 (unimportant) to 3 (critical).

Critical Evaluation

HR can enhance the effectiveness and usefulness of human capital programs by informing their development and monitoring their success, with appropriate data. One such source of data is human capital metrics—for example, metrics that describe the time to fill a position and the cost per hire. Not only do human capital metrics add value to the role of HR in organizations, but HR functions that collect and properly apply HR metrics to inform HR activity are seen as more reliable strategic partners (Lawler, Levenson, & Bourdreau, 2004). The rise of data-based HRM practices is evident—one such example of this trend is "big data" and its increasingly frequent use by HR departments. HR professionals are currently being asked to inform their decisions with data, and this trend is likely to continue and increase in the coming years.

Because of these trends in the HR profession, it is beneficial for HR professionals to have the proficiency necessary to collect, analyze and interpret data and research to inform evidence-based HRM practices. To do this, HR professionals need to understand what data are useful (e.g., HR metrics) and how they should be collected (e.g., surveys, archival records), as well as be able to effectively analyze and interpret those data. In short, HR professionals must be able to translate raw data and research into conclusions relevant to their organizations, and then create actionable recommendations that inform HRM practices. To accomplish these tasks, *Critical Evaluation* is a core competency for HR professionals that is expected to increase in relevance in the coming years.

Critical Evaluation is defined as the ability to interpret information with which to make business decisions and recommendations.

Competency Ratings

Results for *Critical Evaluation* are presented in Table 9.1. This competency was rated as important to the performance of HR professionals (M = 2.1, SD = .65), and 70% of respondents indicated that proficiency in this competency is required upon entry into an HR job. These findings speak to the value of the ability to analyze and interpret data when creating human capital solutions.

Table 9.1. Critical Evaluation: Competency Summary

Rating	Mean *(SD)*
Importance	2.1 *(.65)*
Required upon entry	70%

Key Behaviors

Table 9.2 provides the mean importance ratings of behaviors associated with *Critical Evaluation*. These behaviors reflect the need for HR professionals to gather data (e.g., "Gathers critical information") and analyze and interpret data (e.g., "Analyzes large information to identify evidence-based best practices"). The mean importance scores on the behaviors for *Critical Evaluation* ranged from 1.8 to 2.7, indicating that they are important or critical for successful HR performance.

Table 9.2. Key Behaviors of Critical Evaluation

Key Behaviors	Mean *(SD)*
Makes sound decisions based on evaluation of available information.	2.7 *(.52)*
Assesses the impact of changes to law on organizational human resource management functions.	2.5 *(.64)*
Transfers knowledge and best practices from one situation to the next.	2.4 *(.57)*
Applies critical thinking to information received from organizational stakeholders and evaluates what can be used for organizational success.	2.4 *(.64)*
Gathers critical information.	2.3 *(.63)*
Analyzes data with a keen sense for what is useful.	2.2 *(.59)*
Delineates a clear set of best practices based on experience, evidence from industry literature, published peer-reviewed research, publicly available web-based sources of information and other sources.	2.2 *(.65)*
Analyzes information to identify evidence-based best practices.	2.1 *(.60)*
Identifies leading indicators of outcomes.	2.1 *(.62)*
Analyzes large quantities of information from research and practice.	1.8 *(.68)*

Competency Ratings by Subgroups

Because the importance and necessity of the *Critical Evaluation* competency may differ across demographic and organizational characteristics, more specific analyses of importance and required-upon-entry ratings are presented below.

Career Level

Table 9.3 presents the importance and required-upon-entry ratings for each of the four HR career levels. HR professionals at all career levels indicated that *Critical Evaluation* is important to job success. However, the importance ratings of this competency increase with career level, such that this competency is rated as more important for more senior career levels than for junior career levels. Additionally, more HR professionals indicated that this competency is required upon entering an executive-level job (86%) than an early-career-level job (37%).

These results are consistent with the findings for several other competencies. A large jump in required-upon-entry ratings is seen between the early-career and mid levels, and between the mid and senior levels. This outcome indicates that HR professionals at the early-career and mid levels are expected to develop *Critical Evaluation* through on-the-job experience and formal training opportunities to advance their careers.

Table 9.3. Results by Career Level

Career Level	Importance Mean *(SD)*	Required upon Entry % Yes
Early	1.5 *(.82)*	37
Mid	1.8 *(.65)*	54
Senior	2.2 *(.56)*	77
Executive	2.4 *(.55)*	86

Note: Importance was measured with a 4-point scale ranging from 0 (unimportant) to 3 (critical).

Full-Time Equivalents

Table 9.4 presents the importance and required-upon-entry ratings for *Critical Evaluation* for organizations of varying staff sizes. Although there are minor differences across numbers of FTEs (e.g., between organizations with 1-99 FTEs and organizations with 2,500-24,999 FTEs), these results are generally consistent across organization size. Additionally, ratings suggest that *Critical Evaluation* is important to HR professionals' job success and is required upon entry in most organizations regardless of the number of FTEs.

Table 9.4. Results by Full-Time Equivalents

Full-Time Equivalents	Importance Mean (SD)	Required upon Entry % Yes
1-99	2.1 (.68)	67
100-499	2.2 (.65)	73
500-2,499	2.1 (.65)	70
2,500-24,999	2.2 (.62)	75
>25,000	2.2 (.62)	73

Note: Importance was measured with a 4-point scale ranging from 0 (unimportant) to 3 (critical).

Sector

Table 9.5 presents the importance and required-upon-entry ratings for *Critical Evaluation* for organizations in different sectors. Mean ratings indicate that this competency is important to HR performance and is required upon entry in most organizations. The consistency of these ratings across work sectors indicates that *Critical Evaluation* is important to HR professionals regardless of sector.

Table 9.5. Results by Work Sector

Work Sector	Importance Mean (SD)	Required upon Entry % Yes
For-profit private	2.1 (.66)	69
For-profit public	2.1 (.63)	70
Government	2.2 (.66)	72
Nonprofit	2.2 (.65)	72
Other	2.2 (.65)	71

Note: Importance was measured with a 4-point scale ranging from 0 (unimportant) to 3 (critical).

Business Acumen

HR professionals often serve in a consultative role for other organizational members and business units. This consultative role may include developing and carrying out HRM practices that support, and are aligned with, business strategies and goals. In other words, successful HR professionals develop HR systems that positively contribute to organizational success (Becker & Huselid, 1998).

To do this successfully, HR professionals need to be well developed in terms of their *Business Acumen*. This competency includes understanding business operations and functions, understanding how HRM practices contribute to core business functions, and understanding the organization's external environment. Moreover, HR professionals should also recognize how internal and external factors—for example, the external competitive environment and internal personnel resources—interact to influence organizational performance. Last, HR professionals need to be able to make the case for HR management to other business professionals; this includes marketing HR within the organization and showing how HR can have a direct impact on firm performance.

> *Business Acumen is defined as the ability to understand and apply information with which to contribute to the organization's strategic plan.*

Competency Ratings

Results for *Business Acumen* are presented in Table 10.1. Overall, this competency was rated as important to the performance of HR professionals (M = 2.2, SD = .64), although only 67% of respondents indicated that it is required upon entry. These results are at first somewhat surprising given the influence of well-developed HR systems on organizational performance and the magnitude of the external competitive market on HR-related needs. However, similar to other competencies (e.g., *Consultation*), there are large differences across career levels that limit the utility of making conclusions based on these overall results (discussed further below).

Table 10.1. Business Acumen: Competency Summary

Rating	Mean *(SD)*
Importance	2.2 *(.64)*
Required upon entry	67%

Key Behaviors

The mean importance ratings of behaviors associated with *Business Acumen* are presented in Table 10.2. These behaviors describe HR professionals' need to understand how the organization operates (e.g., "Demonstrates a capacity for understanding the business operations and functions within the organization"), how external factors influence organizational operations (e.g., "Understands the industry and business/competitive environment within which the organization operates"), and how these factors relate to an organization's HR needs (e.g., "Demonstrates an understanding of the strategic relationship between effective human resource management and core business functions"). The mean importance scores on these behaviors reflect important or critical ratings, with mean ratings between 2.0 and 2.5.

Table 10.2. Key Behaviors of Business Acumen

Key Behaviors	Mean *(SD)*
Demonstrates an understanding of the strategic relationship between effective human resource management and core business function.	2.5 *(.58)*
Demonstrates a capacity for understanding the business operations and functions within the organization.	2.5 *(.57)*
Understands the industry and business/competitive environment within which the organization operates.	2.3 *(.62)*
Makes the business case for HR management (e.g., ROI) as it relates to efficient and effective organizational functioning.	2.3 *(.67)*
Uses organizational resources to learn the business and operational functions.	2.3 *(.57)*
Understands organizational metrics and their correlation to business success.	2.3 *(.62)*
Uses organizational metrics to make decisions.	2.1 *(.63)*
Markets HR both internally (e.g., return on investment/ROI of HR initiatives) and externally (e.g., employment branding).	2.1 *(.67)*
Leverages technology to solve business problems.	2.0 *(.61)*

Competency Ratings by Subgroups

Because the importance and necessity of the *Business Acumen* competency may differ across demographic and organizational characteristics, more specific analyses of importance and required-upon-entry ratings are presented below.

Career Level

The importance and required-upon-entry ratings for each of the four HR career levels are presented in Table 10.3. Although HR professionals at all career levels indicated that *Business Acumen* is important or critical to job success, the importance ratings of this competency show important differences across career levels. Specifically, *Business Acumen* was rated as more important for HR professionals at the senior career levels than at the junior career levels. Additionally, there were also marked differences in required-upon-entry ratings across career levels, such that more HR professionals indicated that *Business Acumen* is important upon entering an executive-level job (83%) than an early-career-level job (37%).

Possibly, the job requirements of more junior-career-level employees do not require them to understand the integration of HR with business operations, which would limit the utility of *Business Acumen*. Additionally, employees at junior career levels may be expected to develop this competency through on-the-job training, workshops and other professional development opportunities. On the other hand, HR professionals at the senior and executive levels, who are presumably operating at a more strategic level, need a thorough understanding of the business context to align business goals with HR operations. Despite these career level differences, the data show that this competency is needed both for effective performance as an HR professional and for career advancement.

Table 10.3. Results by Career Level

Career Level	Importance	Required upon Entry
	Mean *(SD)*	% Yes
Early	1.6 *(.75)*	37
Mid	1.9 *(.63)*	51
Senior	2.2 *(.56)*	73
Executive	2.5 *(.54)*	83

Note: Importance was measured with a 4-point scale ranging from 0 (unimportant) to 3 (critical).

Full-Time Equivalents

Table 10.4 presents the importance and required-upon-entry ratings for *Business Acumen* for organizations of varying staff sizes. Across FTE size there were only minimal differences in ratings. These ratings indicate that this competency is important and is required upon entry in a majority of organizations.

Table 10.4. Results by Full-Time Equivalents

Full-Time Equivalents	Importance	Required upon Entry
	Mean *(SD)*	% Yes
1-99	2.1 *(.66)*	66
100-499	2.3 *(.61)*	71
500-2,499	2.1 *(.64)*	67
2,500-24,999	2.3 *(.61)*	70
>25,000	2.2 *(.63)*	68

Note: Importance was measured with a 4-point scale ranging from 0 (unimportant) to 3 (critical).

Sector

Table 10.5 presents the importance and required-upon-entry ratings for *Business Acumen* for organizations in different sectors. As with the number of FTEs, these results show only minimal differences across work sectors. Again, these results indicate that *Business Acumen* is important to HR professionals' job success and is generally required upon entry in all organizations regardless of sector.

Table 10.5. Results by Work Sector

Work Sector	Importance	Required upon Entry
	Mean *(SD)*	% Yes
For-profit private	2.2 *(.66)*	67
For-profit public	2.2 *(.62)*	66
Government	2.1 *(.63)*	64
Nonprofit	2.2 *(.64)*	67
Other	2.2 *(.65)*	70

Note: Importance was measured with a 4-point scale ranging from 0 (unimportant) to 3 (critical).

Summary

Based on an extensive review of the academic and professional literature, as well as over 100 focus groups with HR professionals around the world, SHRM developed the SHRM Competency Model. This model comprises nine competencies—one technical and eight behavioral—that describe the requisite personal characteristics (i.e., competencies) of successful HR professionals. A particular benefit of SHRM's model is that it is not organization-specific, but is instead intended for the entire HR profession regardless of job specialty, career level and other personal or organizational differences.

Although the SHRM Competency Model was built based on the input of thousands of HR professionals, the purpose of this study was to confirm the content of the model. SHRM deployed a large-scale survey of more than 32,000 HR professionals for this purpose. Respondents to this survey rated the importance of each competency and its need upon entry into an HR job. Additionally, information about the respondents' demographic and organizational characteristics was collected to investigate subgroup differences in ratings.

Results of this survey indicate that the competencies and key behaviors included in the SHRM Competency Model are not only important for job success as an HR professional but are often a prerequisite for entry into an HR job. An analysis of these findings across career levels indicates that whereas all of these competencies are important regardless of career level, they are especially important for more senior-level HR professionals. A similar pattern of results was also found for the required-upon-entry ratings, indicating that more senior-level HR professionals are expected to be well developed in each of these competencies. Taken together, these findings demonstrate the value of these competencies to the HR profession. Additionally, these findings, specifically the differences across career levels, provide a clear developmental path for early-career HR professionals who wish to advance their careers. Lastly, only minimal differences in ratings were found across organizational size and work sector. These relatively invariant results speak to the universal nature of the model.

In summary, the findings presented here regarding the importance and requirement upon entry of these competencies for HR professionals provide strong evidence of the applicability of the competency model to the HR profession. Additionally, the high importance ratings assigned to the key behaviors associated with each competency confirm the importance of these behaviors to their respective competencies. Taken together, these findings provide strong support for the content validity of the SHRM Competency Model and its applicability to the entire HR profession.

References

Allen, T. D., Eby, L. T., Poteet, M. L., Lentz, E., & Lima, L. (2004). Career benefits associated with mentoring for protégés: A meta-analysis. *Journal of Applied Psychology, 89*, 127-136.

Alvesson, M., & Sveningsson, S. (2003). Managers doing leadership: The extra-ordinarization of the mundane. *Human Relations, 56*, 1435-1459.

Barling, J., Christie, A., & Hoption, A. (2010). Leadership. In S. Zedeck (Ed.), *Handbook of industrial and organizational psychology* (pp. 183-240). Washington, DC: American Psychological Association.

Bartels, L. K., Harrick, E., Martell, K., & Strickland, D. (1998). The relationship between ethical climate and ethical problems within human resource management. *Journal of Business Ethics, 17*, 799-804.

Becker, B., & Gerhart, B. (1996). The impact of human resource management on organizational performance: Progress and prospects. *Academy of Management Journal, 39*, 779-801.

Becker B. E., & Huselid, M.A. (1998). High performance work systems and firm performance: A synthesis of research and managerial implications. In G. R. Ferris (Ed.), *Research in personnel and human resources management* (pp. 53-101). Stamford, CT: JAI Press.

Berman, E. M., West, J. P., & Richter, M. N. (2002). Workplace relations: Friendship patterns and consequences (according to managers). *Public Administration Review, 62*, 217-230.

Burke, C. S., Sims, D. E., Lazzara, E. H., & Salas, E. (2007). Trust in leadership: A multi-level review and integration. *The Leadership Quarterly, 18*, 606-632.

Campion, M. A., Fink, A. A., Ruggeberg, B. J., Carr, L., Phillips, G. M., & Odman, R. B. (2011). Doing competencies well: Best practices in competency modeling. *Personnel Psychology, 64*, 225-262.

Combs, J., Liu, Y., Hall, A., & Ketchen, D. (2006). How much do high-performance work practices matter? A meta-analysis of their effects on organizational performance. *Personnel Psychology, 59*, 501-528.

Den Hartog, D. N., Boon, C., Verburg, R. M., & Croon, M. A. (2013). HRM, communication, satisfaction, and perceived performance: A cross-level test. *Journal of Management, 39*, 1637-1665.

Huselid, M. A. (1995). The impact of human resource management practices on turnover, productivity, and corporate financial performance. *Academy of Management Journal, 38*, 635-672.

Jayne, M. E. A., & Dipboye, R. L. (2004). Leveraging diversity to improve business performance: Research findings and recommendations for organizations. *Human Resource Management, 43*, 409-424.

Judge, T. A., & Piccolo, R. F. (2004). Transformational and transactional leadership: A meta-analytic test of their relative validity. *Journal of Applied Psychology, 89*, 755-768.

Kimley, A. (1997). Diversity programs: Coming of age. *Black Enterprise Magazine, 4.*

References

Kristof-Brown, A. L., Zimmerman, R. D., & Johnson, E. C. (2005). Consequences of individuals' fit at work: A meta-analysis of person-job, person-organization, person-group, and person-supervisor fit. *Personnel Psychology, 58*, 281-342.

Kulik, C. T., & Roberson, L. (2008). Common goals and golden opportunities: A research agenda for diversity education in academic and organizational settings. *Academy of Management Learning and Education, 7*, 309-331.

Lado, A. A., & Wilson, M. C. (1994). Human resource systems and sustained competitive advantage: A competency-based perspective. *Academy of Management Review, 19*, 699-727.

Lawler III, E. E., Levenson, A., & Boudreau, J. W. (2004). HR metric and analytics: Use and impact. *Resource Planning, 27*, 27-35.

Pfeffer, J. (1998). Seven practices of successful organizations. *California Management Review, 40*, 96-124.

Reich, T. C., & Hershcovis, M. S. (2011). Interpersonal relationships at work. In S. Zedeck, H. Aguinis, W. Cascio, M. Gelfand, K. Leung, S. Parker, & J. Zhou (Eds.), *Handbook of industrial and organizational psychology* (Vol. 3, pp. 223-248). Washington, DC: American Psychological Association.

Shippmann, J. S., Ash, R. A., Battista, M., Carr, L., Eyde, L. D., Hesketh, B., Kehoe, J., Pearlman, K., Prien, E.P., & Sanchez, J. I. (2000). The practice of competency modeling. *Personnel Psychology, 53*, 703-740.

Showry, M. M., & Manasa, K. (2012). Effective communication for professional excellence. *IUP Journal of Soft Skills, 6*, 39-46.

Wallace, J. C., Edwards, B. D., Arnold T., Frazier, M. L., & Finch, D. M. (2009). Work stressors, role-based performance, and the moderating influence of organizational support. *Journal of Applied Psychology, 94*, 254-262.

Appendix: Summary of Competency Importance and Required-upon-Entry Ratings by Career Level

Competency	Early • Is a specialist in a specific support function, or is a generalist with limited experience • Holds a title such as HR assistant, junior recruiter or benefits clerk		Mid • Is a generalist or a senior specialist • Manages projects or programs • Holds a title such as HR manager, generalist or senior specialist		Senior • Is a very experienced generalist or specialist • Holds a title such as senior manager, director or principal		Executive • Typically is one of the most senior leaders in HR • Holds the top HR job in the organization or VP role	
	IMP (SD)	RUE (%)	IMP (SD)	RUE (%)	IMP (SD)	RUE (%)	IMP (SD)	RUE (%)
Ethical Practice The ability to integrate core values, integrity and accountability throughout all organizational and business practices	2.5 (.62)	90	2.6 (.52)	95	2.8 (.44)	97	2.9 (.35)	98
Relationship Management The ability to manage interactions to provide service and to support the organization	2.1 (.65)	73	2.3 (.57)	86	2.6 (.52)	94	2.7 (.47)	96
Human Resource Expertise (HR Knowledge) The knowledge of principles, practices, and functions of effective human resource management	1.8 (.74)	44	2.2 (.55)	86	2.7 (.50)	95	2.8 (.43)	94

continued on next page

Appendix

Competency	Early • Is a specialist in a specific support function, or is a generalist with limited experience • Holds a title such as HR assistant, junior recruiter or benefits clerk		Mid • Is a generalist or a senior specialist • Manages projects or programs • Holds a title such as HR manager, generalist or senior specialist		Senior • Is a very experienced generalist or specialist • Holds a title such as senior manager, director or principal		Executive • Typically is one of the most senior leaders in HR • Holds the top HR job in the organization or VP role	
	IMP *(SD)*	RUE (%)	IMP *(SD)*	RUE (%)	IMP *(SD)*	RUE (%)	IMP *(SD)*	RUE (%)
Communication The ability to effectively exchange information with stakeholders	2.1 *(.72)*	77	2.3 *(.61)*	85	2.5 *(.54)*	93	2.6 *(.50)*	95
Consultation The ability to provide guidance to organizational stakeholders	1.5 *(.85)*	34	2.1 *(.66)*	67	2.4 *(.56)*	89	2.6 *(.53)*	91
Leadership and Navigation The ability to direct and contribute to initiatives and processes within the organization	1.3 *(.87)*	24	1.7 *(.70)*	41	2.3 *(.58)*	78	2.6 *(.51)*	90
Business Acumen The ability to understand and apply information with which to contribute to the organization's strategic plan	1.6 *(.75)*	37	1.9 *(.63)*	51	2.2 *(.56)*	73	2.5 *(.54)*	83
Critical Evaluation The ability to interpret information with which to make business decisions and recommendations	1.5 *(.82)*	37	1.8 *(.65)*	54	2.2 *(.56)*	77	2.4 *(.55)*	86
Global and Cultural Effectiveness The ability to value and consider the perspectives and backgrounds of all parties	1.5 *(.87)*	41	1.7 *(.75)*	47	2.0 *(.65)*	60	2.1 *(.63)*	66

Note: IMP = mean importance rating; SD = standard deviation; RUE = required-upon-entry rating. Importance was measured with a 4-point scale ranging from 0 (unimportant) to 3 (critical).

Endnotes

Part I

1. Keith H. Hammonds, "Why We Hate HR," *Fast Company*, August 2005, http://www.fastcompany.com/53319/ why-we-hate-hr; and Ram Charan, "It's Time to Split HR," *Harvard Business Review*, July 2014, https://hbr. org/2014/07/its-time-to-split-hr.
2. American Institutes for Research, "Society for Human Resource Management's State of Human Resource Education Study: 2013 HR Faculty Survey Final Technical Report," November 15, 2013, http://www.shrm.org/Education/ hreducation/Documents/2013%20SOHRE_HR%20Faculty%20Study_Tech%20Report_%20FINAL_External%20Version_BS_12%2015%202013_SG.pdf.

Chapter 1

1. Jeffery S. Shippmann et al, "The Practice of Competency Modeling," *Personnel Psychology* 53, no. 3 (September 2000): 703-740; and Michael A. Campion et al, "Doing Competencies Well: Best Practices in Competency Modeling," *Personnel Psychology* 64, no. 1 (Spring 2011): 225-262.
2. George A. Miller, "The Magical Number Seven, Plus or Minus Two: Some Limits on Our Capacity for Processing Informa-

tion," *The Psychological Review* 63, no. 2 (March 1956): 81-97; Donna Blancero et al, "Key Competencies for a Transformed Human Resource Organization: Results of a Field Study," *Human Resource Management* 35, no. 3 (Fall 1996): 383-403.

3. David C. McClelland, "Testing for Competence Rather Than for 'Intelligence'," *American Psychologist* 28 no. 1 (January 1973): 1-14.

4. Richard E. Boyatzis, *The Competent Manager: A Model for Effective Performance* (New York: John Wiley, 1982).

5. Shippmann et al., "The Practice of Competency Modeling."

6. C. K. Prahalad and Gary Hamel, "The Core Competence of the Corporation," *Harvard Business Review* 68, no. 3 (May 1990): 79-91, https://hbr.org/1990/05/the-core-competence-of-the-corporation.

7. Deloitte, "Talent Edge 2020: Blueprints for the New Normal," December 2010, http://www.deloitte.com/assets/dcom-unitedstates/local%20assets/documents/imos/talent/us_talent-edge2020_121710.pdf.

8. Daniel Katz and Robert L. Kahn, *The Social Psychology of Organizations*, 2nd ed. (New York: Wiley, 1978).

9. Dave Ulrich et al, *HR Competencies: Mastery at the Intersection of People and Business* (Alexandria, VA: Society for Human Resource Management, 2008).

10. Tom E. Lawson and Vaughan Limbrick, "Critical Competencies and Developmental Experiences for Top HR Executives," *Human Resource Management* 35, no. 1 (Spring 1996): 67-85.

11. Patrick M. Wright et al (eds) , *The Chief HR Officer: Defining the New Role of Human Resource Leaders* (San Francisco, CA: Jossey-Bass, 2011).

12. Such as Dave Ulrich et al, "Human Resource Competencies: An Empirical Assessment," *Human Resource Management* 34, no. 4 (Winter 1995): 473-496; Stephen C. Schoonover, *Human Resource Competencies for the Year 2000: The Wake-Up Call!* (Alexandria VA: SHRM Foundation, 1998); and Stephen

C. Schoonover, *Human Resource Competencies for the New Century* (Falmouth, MA: Schoonover Associates, 2003).

13. Michael A. Campion et al, "Doing Competencies Well; and Shippmann et al., "The Practice of Competency Modeling."

14. Thomas H. W. Ng and Daniel C. Feldman, "How Broadly Does Education Affect Performance?" *Personnel Psychology* 62 (2009):89-34; and Philip L. Roth et al,, "Meta-analyzing the Relationship between Grades and Job Performance," *Journal of Applied Psychology* 81, no. 5 (October 1996): 548-556.

15. Anntoinette D. Lucia and Richard Lepsinger, *The Art and Science of Competency Models: Pinpointing Critical Success Factors in Organizations* (San Francisco: Jossey-Bass/Pfeiffer, 1999).

16. Campion et al., "Doing Competencies Well."

17. Ibid.

18. See Michael A. Campion et al, "Doing Competencies Well; and Jeffery S. Shippmann, "The Practice of Competency Modeling.

19. Uniform Guidelines on Employee Selection Procedures (1978), 29 C.F.R. § 1607, http://www.gpo.gov/fdsys/pkg/CFR-2013-title29-vol4/xml/CFR-2013-title29-vol4-part1607.xml; U.S. Equal Employment Opportunity Commission, "Adoption of Questions and Answers To Clarify and Provide a Common Interpretation of the Uniform Guidelines on Employee Selection Procedures," Federal Register 44 no. 43 (March 2, 1979), http://www.eeoc.gov/policy/docs/qanda_clarify_procedures.html.

20. Society for Industrial and Organizational Psychology, Principles for the Validation and Use of Personnel Selection Procedures, 4th ed. (Bowling Green, OH: Author, 2003), http://www.siop.org/_Principles/principles.pdf.

21. "SHRM Competency Model: Criterion Validation Report," Society for Human Resource Management, 2015.

Chapter 2

1. Jeffrey Pfeffer, "Seven Practices of Successful Organizations," *California Management Review* 40, no. 2 (Winter 1998): 96-124.
2. Brian Becker and Barry Gerhart, "The Impact of Human Resource Management on Organizational Performance: Progress and Prospects," *Academy of Management Journal* 39, no. 4 (1996): 779-801; and Mark A. Huselid, "The Impact of Human Resource Management Practices on Turnover, Productivity, and Corporate Financial Performance," *Academy of Management Journal* 38, no. 3 (1995): 635-672.
3. For more information about SHRM's certifications, please visit http://www.shrmcertification.org.

Chapter 3

1. Augustine A. Lado and Mary C. Wilson, "Human Resource Systems and Sustained Competitive Advantage: A Competency-Based Perspective," *Academy of Management Review* 19, no. 4 (1994): 699-727.

Chapter 5

1. Edward E. Lawler III et al, "HR Metrics and Analytics: Use and Impact," *Human Resource Planning* 27, no. 4 (October 2004): 27-35.
2. Ibid.

Chapter 6

1. Brian E. Becker and Mark A. Huselid, "High Performance Work Systems and Firm Performance: A Synthesis of Research and Managerial Implications," in *Research in Personnel and*

Human Resources Management, ed. Gerald R. Ferris (Stamford, CT: JAI Press, 1998), 53-101.

2. James Combs et al, "How Much Do High-Performance Work Practices Matter? A Meta-Analysis of Their Effects on Organizational Performance," *Personnel Psychology* 59, no. 3 (Autumn 2006): 501-528.

Part IV

1. A team-based structure is a type of organizational structure that allows autonomous, semi-autonomous, or cross-functional teams to work in a way that allows them to be more effective in meeting goals. They have their own budgets, can hire and fire team members, etc.

Chapter 7

1. Tara C. Reich and M. Sandy Hershcovis, "Interpersonal Relationships at Work," in *APA Handbook of Industrial and Organizational Psychology,* ed. Sheldon Zedeck (Washington, DC: American Psychological Association, 2011), 3: 223-248.

2. Mats Alvesson and Stefan Sveningsson, "Managers Doing Leadership: The Extra-Ordinarization of the Mundane," *Human Relations* 56, no. 12 (December 2003): 1435-1459.

3. Tammy D. Allen et al, "Career Benefits Associated with Mentoring for Protégés: A Meta-Analysis," *Journal of Applied Psychology* 89, no. 1 (February 2004): 127-136.

4. Evan M. Berman et al, "Workplace Relations: Friendship Patterns and Consequences (According to Managers)," *Public Administration Review* 62, no. 2 (March-April 2002): 217-230.

5. J. Craig Wallace et al, "Work Stressors, Role-Based Performance, and the Moderating Influence of Organizational Support," *Journal of Applied Psychology* 94, no. 1 (January 2009): 254-262.

6. Amy L. Kristof-Brown et al, "Consequences of Individuals' Fit at Work: A Meta-Analysis of Person-Job, Person-Organization, Person-Group, and Person-Supervisor Fit," *Personnel Psychology* 58 (June 2): 281-342.

7. The O*Net OnLine website is at http://www.onetonline.org. O*NET OnLine is sponsored by the U.S. Department of Labor, Employment & Training Administration, and developed by the National Center for O*NET Development.

8. Rachel Morrison, "Informal Relationships in the Workplace: Associations with Job Satisfaction, Organisational Commitment and Turnover Intentions," *New Zealand Journal of Psychology*, 33 no. 3 (November 2004): 114-128; and Stephen J. Zaccaro and M. Catherine McCoy, "The Effects of Task and Interpersonal Cohesiveness on Performance of a Disjunctive Group Task," *Journal of Applied Social Psychology*, 18 no. 10 (August 1988): 837-851.

Chapter 8

1. Gary A. Yukl, *Leadership in Organizations*, 8th ed. (San Francisco, Jossey-Bass, 2012); and Paul M. Muchinsky, *Psychology Applied at Work*, 8th ed. (Stamford, CT: Wadsworth, 2005).

2. Yukl, *Leadership in Organizations*.

3. Edwin A. Fleishman, "Performance Assessment Based on an Empirically Derived Task Taxonomy," *Human Factors* 9, no. 4 (August 1967): 349-366.

4. Fred E. Fiedler, "A Contingency Model of Leadership Effectiveness," in *Advances in Experimental Social Psychology*, ed. Leonard Berkowitz (New York: McGraw-Hill, 1964), 149-190; Martin G. Evans, "The Effects of Supervisory Behavior on the Path-Goal Relationship," *Organizational Behavior and Human Performance*, 5 no. 3 (May 1970): 277-298; Steven Kerr and John M. Jermier, "Substitutes for Leadership: Their Meaning and Measurement," *Organizational Behavior and Human Per-*

formance, 22 no. 3 (December 1978): 375-403; Yukl, *Leadership in Organizations;* and Fred E. Fiedler, "The Contribution of Cognitive Resources to Leadership Performance," *Journal of Applied Social Psychology,* 16 no. 6 (September 1986): 532-548.

5. Ben B. Morgan Jr. and Donald L. Lassiter, "Team Composition and Staffing," in *Teams: Their Training and Performance,* ed. Robert W. Swezey and Eduardo Salas (Norwood, NJ: Ablex, 1992), 75-100; and Yukl, *Leadership in Organizations.*

6. James MacGregor Burns, *Leadership* (New York: HarperCollins, 1978); Bernard M. Bass, *A New Paradigm of Leadership: An Inquiry into Transformational Leadership* (Alexandria, VA: U.S. Army Research Institute for the Behavioral and Social Sciences, 1996); and Bernard M. Bass and Bruce J. Avolio, *Transformational Leadership Development: Manual for the Multifactor Leadership Questionnaire* (Palo Alto, CA: Consulting Psychologists Press, 1990).

7. Bernard M. Bass, *A New Paradigm of Leadership.*

8. Edwin A. Locke and Gary P. Latham, *A Theory of Goal Setting and Task Performance* (Englewood Cliffs, NJ: Prentice Hall, 1990).

Chapter 9

1. Mendemu Showry and K.V.L. Manasa, "Effective Communication for Professional Excellence," *IUP Journal of Soft Skills,* 6 no. 1 (March 2012): 39-46.

2. Deanne N. Den Hartog et al, "HRM, Communication, Satisfaction, and Perceived Performance: A Cross-Level Test," *Journal of Management* 39, no. 6 (September 2013): 1637-1665.

3. Ibid.

4. Bradley L. Kirkman et al, "Five Challenges to Virtual Team Success: Lessons from Sabre, Inc.," *Academy of Management Executive* 16, no. 3 (August 2002): 67-79.

Chapter 10

1. See the "Key Behaviors" under the *Global and Cultural Effectiveness* competency in Appendix B.
2. Ibid.

Chapter 11

1. Edwin A. Locke and Gary P. Latham, *A Theory of Goal Setting and Task Performance* (Englewood Cliffs, NJ: Prentice-Hall, 1990).
2. Interview with one of the authors.

Chapter 12

1. See the "Key Behaviors" under the *Leadership and Navigation* competency in Appendix B.
2. For more information about the SHRM Diagnostic™—*Self Tool*, visit http://www.shrm.org/hrcompetencies/pages/self-assessment.aspx.

Chapter 13

1. David C. McClelland, "Testing for Competence Rather than for 'Intelligence,'" *American Psychologist*, 28, no. 1 (January 1973): 1-14.
2. John E. Hunter and Ronda F. Hunter, "Validity and Utility of Alternative Predictors of Job Performance," *Psychological Bulletin* 96, no. 1 (July 1984): 72-98; Frank Schmidt and John E. Hunter, "The Validity and Utility of Selection Methods in Personnel Psychology: Practical and Theoretical Implications of 85 Years of Research Findings," *Psychological Bulletin* 124, no. 2 (September 1998): 262-274; and Kevin R. Murphy, ed.,

Validity Generalization: A Critical Review (Mahwah, NJ: Lawrence Erlbaum Associates, 2003)

3. Melvin G. Villeme, "Competency-Based Certification: A New Reality?" *Educational Leadership* 31, no. 4 (January 1974): 348-349.

4. For more information regarding SHRM certifications, please visit http://www.shrmcertification.org.

Chapter 14

1. Quotes in this chapter are based on a series of interviews conducted by one of the authors.

Index

About the Authors

Kari R. Strobel, Ph.D., is the Society for Human Resource Management's (SHRM's) Director for HR Competencies and is responsible for leading all research activities to support the maintenance, validation, and implementation of SHRM's Competency Model. She oversees the development of competency-based products to include developmental assessments and selection tools, and the research to support the update of the competency model, which provides the foundation for professional development and certification for global HR professionals. She is also responsible for advancing SHRM's workforce analytics program, supporting the identification critical HR trends and enhancing SHRM's position as an authority on HR metrics and the application of statistical models to worker-related data to optimize human resource management. Prior to joining SHRM, Dr. Strobel worked at the Office of the Secretary of Defense where she was responsible for leading competency-based strategic human capital planning for the Department of Defense Total Force. Here she directed the development and assessment of competencies, the analysis of skill gaps, and forecasting for mission critical occupations. Dr. Strobel has been responsible for directing organizational development projects for the United States Navy's Surface Warfare Enterprise to include Commander Naval Surface Forces, Naval Mine and Anti-submarine Warfare Command, and the Center for Personal and Professional Development. Dr. Strobel received her Doctor of Philosophy degree in Industrial-Organizational Psychology from Old Dominion University, and has demonstrated success in competency-based performance, strategic human resource planning, team performance improvement, organizational change, and talent management. With numerous journal articles, technical reports, and national and international conference presentations, to include published works in *Journal of Applied Psychology* and *Human Performance, Situation Awareness and Automation*, Dr. Strobel has received national recognition for her contributions to the field. She was the first recipient of the American Psychological Association Division 19 (Military Psychology) Research Award, and received Honorable Mention from the Virginia Academy of Science for her longitudinal team cohesion and performance research.

James N. Kurtessis, MA, is the manager of validation research for SHRM's certification programs. At SHRM he has been responsible for collecting and evaluating validity evidence for SHRM's HR Competency Model and other competency based products and has worked on the development of SHRM's certification exams. Prior to SHRM, he worked at the American Institutes for Research where his work included the development and validation of employee selection systems and performance appraisal instruments, the evaluation of training programs, job analyses, and the development and analysis of surveys. He has published works in peer-reviewed journals such as the *Journal of Management* and *Organizational Research Methods*. He has also been active in the professional community, serving on the board of the Personnel Testing Council of Metropolitan Washington since 2011, as chair of the accreditation committee for the International Personnel Assessment Council, and as a member of the Society for Industrial and Organizational Psychology's Professional Practice committee.

Debra J. Cohen, Ph.D., SHRM-SCP is senior vice president, knowledge development, for the Society for Human Resource

Management (SHRM) and is responsible for the Society's Knowledge Development Division which includes the SHRM Knowledge Center (including the Society Library), the Research Department, Academic Initiatives, and HR Competencies. Prior to joining SHRM, Dr. Cohen spent 15 years as an academician teaching HRM at George Washington University (10 years) and George Mason University (5 years). Dr. Cohen has published over 40 articles and book chapters and has been published in such journals as *Academy of Management Journal, Personnel Psychology, Human Resource Development Quarterly, Journal of Management, Human Resource Management,* and others. She is co-editor of the book *Developing and Enhancing High-Performing Teams: Evidence Practices and Advice.*

Dr. Cohen sits on the Business Practices Council for AACSB International, the Association to Advancement of Collegiate Schools of Business, is a frequent presenter both nationally and internationally and is often quoted in the media. Dr. Cohen received her Ph.D. in Management and Human Resources and her Master's Degree in Labor and Human Resources (MLHR) both from The Ohio State University. She received her Bachelor of Science (in Communications) from Ohio University. Prior to her academic career, she was a practicing Human Resources Manager (in Training and Development).

Alexander Alonso, Ph.D., SHRM-SCP is the Society for Human Resource Management's (SHRM's) Vice President for Research and currently serves as the head of examination development and operations for SHRM's Certified Professional and Senior Certified Professional certifications. He is responsible for all research activities including the development of the SHRM Competency Model. He oversees the teams responsible for research products like People Insight engagement tools, SHRM Benchmarking Services, and the Workplace and Employment Trends Center. During his career, he has worked with numerous subject matter experts worldwide with the aim of identifying performance standards, developing competency models, designing organizational assessments, and conducting job analyses. He was also responsible for working on contract task orders involving the development of measurement tools for content areas such as job knowledge (like teacher knowledge of instructional processes) and organizational climates (like organizational climate forecasting in military health care). He possesses experience in projects dealing with organizational assessments and workforce analysis drawing on interdisciplinary advanced training, quantitative and qualitative research methods, as well as multicultural and foreign language skills. Dr. Alonso received his doctorate in Industrial-Organizational Psychology from Florida International University in 2003. Dr. Alonso was part of the team recognized by the Society for Industrial Organizational Psychology (Division 14 of the APA; SIOP) with the 2007 M. Scott Myers Award for Applied Research in the Workplace for the development of the federal standard for medical team training, TeamSTEPPS. In addition, Dr. Alonso was awarded a 2009 Presidential Citation for Innovative Practice by the American Psychological Association for supporting the development of competency model for team triage in emergency medicine. He is also the recipient of the 2013 SIOP Distinguished Early Career Contributions for Practice Award. He has published works in peer-reviewed journals such as *Journal of Applied Psychology, International Journal of Selection and Assessment, Personality and Individual Differences, Quality and Safety in Health Care,* and *Human Resources Management Review.* Dr. Alonso also served as a columnist reviewing international practice topics for *The Industrial Psychologist* from 2011-2014. He has also served as the Chairperson for the SIOP International Affairs Committee, a member of the SIOP Professional Practice, Awards, and Program Committees, and the 2014 president of the Personnel Testing Council of Metropolitan Washington. He currently serves as the SIOP Executive Board Communications Portfolio Officer.

A Sampling of SHRM-Published Books that Support the SHRM Competency Model

Business Acumen

The ACE Advantage: How Smart Companies Unleash Talent for Optimal Performance
William A. Schiemann

Business-Focused HR: 11 Processes to Drive Results
Scott P. Mondore, Shane S. Douthitt, and Marisa A. Carson

Communication

A Necessary Evil: Managing Employee Activity on Facebook, Twitter, LinkedIn . . . and the Hundreds of Other Social Media Sites
Aliah D. Wright

Up, Down, and Sideways: High-Impact Verbal Communication for HR Professionals
Patricia M. Buhler and Joel D. Worden

Consultation

Got a Solution? HR Approaches to 5 Common and Persistent Business Problems
Dale J. Dwyer and Sheri A. Caldwell

HR's Greatest Challenge: Driving the C-Suite to Improve Employee Engagement and Retention
Richard P. Finnegan

Critical Evaluation

Becoming the Evidence-Based Manager: Making the Science of Management Work for You
Gary P. Latham

Repurposing HR: From a Cost Center to a Business Accelerator
Carol E. M. Anderson

Ethical Practice

Give Your Company a Fighting Chance: An HR Guide to Understanding and Preventing Workplace Violence
Maria Greco Danaher

Stop Bullying at Work: Strategies and Tools for HR and Legal Professionals
Teresa A. Daniel and Gary S. Metcalf

Global and Cultural Effectiveness

Leading with Your Heart: Diversity and Ganas for Inspired Inclusion
Cari M. Dominguez and Judith Sotherlund

Transformational Diversity: Why and How Intercultural Competencies Can Help Organizations to Survive and Thrive
Fiona Citkin and Lynda Spielman

HR Expertise

From Hello to Goodbye: Proactive Tips for Maintaining Positive Employee Relations
Christine V. Walters

The Power of Stay Interviews for Engagement and Retention
Richard P. Finnegan

Leadership and Navigation

Destination Innovation: HR's Role in Charting the Course
    Patricia M. Buhler

Hidden Drivers of Success: Leveraging Employee Insights for
    Strategic Advantage
    William A. Schiemann, Jerry H. Seibert, and Brian S. Morgan

Relationship Management

HR at Your Service: Lessons from Benchmark Service Organizations
    Gary P. Latham and Robert C. Ford

Human Resource Essentials: Your Guide to Starting and Running
    the HR Function
    Lin Grensing-Pophal

For a comprehensive list of titles, please visit
http://www.shrm.org/publications/books/pages/shrm-
competencies-library.aspx.